"This book is a must-read primer cultivate and develop school leade. from practicing principals across the country, readers will learn what excellent preparation programs look like and the policies to create them in their communities for a diverse set of learners."

Ronn Nozoe, *Chief Executive Officer, National Association of Secondary School Principals*

"This book is a comprehensive and eminently readable synthesis of research about the features of high quality initial and ongoing educational leadership development programs in the US. Without doubt, it is the most authoritative source of guidance currently available to policy makers, leadership developers, and individual leaders searching for the most productive ways of improving their own practice."

Kenneth Leithwood, *author of* How Leadership Influences Student Learning

"*Developing Expert Principals* is being published at just the right time! This book advances a research-based theory of action for principal development that is supported with powerful illustrations from a variety of high-quality programs and learning experiences in diverse settings across the US. My hope is that this book will be widely considered by those who seek to continuously improve programs for principal preparation and development as well as by those who advance policies to impact these aims."

Shelby Cosner, *Professor of Educational Organization and Leadership and Director of the Center for Urban Education Leadership at University of Illinois, Chicago*

"We know that pandemic-era demands such as increased attention to the mental health needs of students and staff and crisis management led principals to prioritize specific professional skills over others. Yet, as principals continue to lead schools through recovery, their professional learning and support are more important than ever. *Developing Expert Principals* shines a critical light on the elements of high-quality professional learning that can produce positive school outcomes."

L. Earl Franks, *Executive Director, National Association of Elementary School Principals*

DEVELOPING EXPERT PRINCIPALS

Strong school leadership is critical for shaping engaging learning environments, supporting high-quality teachers and teaching, and influencing student outcomes. *Developing Expert Principals* offers a comprehensive research synthesis to understand the elements of high-quality programs and learning experiences that have been associated with positive outcomes ranging from principals' preparedness and practices to staff retention and student achievement. This book also offers vivid examples of high-quality programs and examines the extent to which principals have opportunities to participate in effective learning experiences. It examines the policies that drive both the development of high-quality programs and access to them, highlighting successful examples across the country. With practical recommendations throughout, this book is a key resource for educational leaders, faculty and scholars of educational leadership, developers of leadership preparation and training, and policymakers who seek to create a learning system that will better serve principals, the staff they support, and, ultimately, all children.

Linda Darling-Hammond is Professor of Education Emeritus at Stanford University and President of the Learning Policy Institute, USA. She is a past President of AERA and author of *Preparing School Leaders for a Changing World*.

Marjorie E. Wechsler is Principal Research Manager at the Learning Policy Institute, USA, and author of *Preparing Leaders for Deeper Learning*.

Stephanie Levin is Research Manager at the Learning Policy Institute, USA, and author of *Understanding and Addressing Principal Turnover*.

Melanie Leung-Gagné is Research and Policy Associate on the Educator Quality and Equitable Resources and Access teams at the Learning Policy Institute, USA.

Steven Tozer is Professor Emeritus of Educational Policy Studies at University of Illinois, Chicago, founding Director of the UIC Center for Urban Education Leadership, and founding Coordinator of the UIC Ed.D. Program in Urban Education Leadership, USA.

Ayana Kee Campoli is Educator for the Dekalb County, Georgia, School District and former Senior Researcher for the Learning Policy Institute, USA.

DEVELOPING EXPERT PRINCIPALS

Professional Learning that Matters

Linda Darling-Hammond, Marjorie E. Wechsler,
Stephanie Levin, Melanie Leung-Gagné,
Steven Tozer, and Ayana Kee Campoli

Routledge
Taylor & Francis Group

NEW YORK AND LONDON

Designed cover image: © Getty Images

First published 2024
by Routledge
605 Third Avenue, New York, NY 10158

and by Routledge
4 Park Square, Milton Park, Abingdon, Oxon, OX14 4RN

Routledge is an imprint of the Taylor & Francis Group, an informa business

© 2024 Learning Policy Institute

The right of Linda Darling-Hammond, Marjorie E. Wechsler, Stephanie Levin, Melanie Leung-Gagné, Steven Tozer, and Ayana Kee Campoli to be identified as authors of this work has been asserted in accordance with sections 77 and 78 of the Copyright, Designs and Patents Act 1988.

ISBN: 978-1-032-46182-3 (hbk)
ISBN: 978-1-032-46181-6 (pbk)
ISBN: 978-1-003-38045-0 (ebk)

DOI: 10.4324/9781003380450

Typeset in Galliard
by Apex CoVantage, LLC

Portions of this book have been reprinted and adapted with permission from Wechsler, M. E., & Wojcikiewicz, S. K. (2023). *Preparing leaders for deeper learning*. Harvard Education Press. Copyright (c) 2023 by the President and Fellows of Harvard College.

CONTENTS

TABLES

FIGURES

PREFACE

This book originated in the extraordinary three-decade quest of the Wallace Foundation to understand and support the development of school leadership that enables high-quality learning environments for all children and youth. Whereas many foundations cycle through a range of different topics that come and go over relatively short periods of time, Wallace defined a critically important field before most recognized its importance; invested in and consolidated a continuing body of research to understand ever more fully what matters in the preparation and support of educational leaders; launched field efforts to build programs and policies based on this research in partnership with states, local districts, and universities; studied the outcomes; and took up the new questions that emerged for further study and development. In this way the Foundation has helped to build a knowledge base, as well as a policy and practice base, for strengthened principal development programs across the country.

This study was part of that iterative process. More than two decades ago, a number of studies established that principals' leadership behaviors—including their focus on instruction and school climate, as well as their ability to set a vision and manage change—influence a range of school conditions and student outcomes. Wallace supported and synthesized much of this research and sponsored a study of principal development, seeking to discover how these behaviors can be consciously developed by preservice and in-service programs for principals. One of the authors of this book led a study, *Preparing Principals for a Changing World,* that found a number of commonalities among highly effective principal development programs—and also found that principals who participated in such programs felt more

efficacious, less stressed by their roles (even in high-need urban communities), and more likely to plan to stay in the principalship. The study also
documented some of the policies that were used in states committed to
developing stronger programs and learning opportunities.

The Wallace Foundation and others used the growing body of research to
support reforms of policy and practice in states and districts across the country. While there was a time when principal certification programs focused on
administrative matters like budgets and bus schedules, often in late-night
classes teachers took after working all day, they began to use the new knowledge base to focus instead on how school leaders could influence the core
practices of schools, develop staff, and ensure quality instruction. The new
knowledge base also pointed to the importance of designing and funding
programs that could proactively recruit promising individuals into opportunities to work under the mentorship of expert principals while learning how
to engage in leadership directly, rather than only imagining how to do so.
Over the subsequent decade and a half, a growing number of states enacted
standards for principal licensing and program accreditation that embodied
this new vision, and many more programs took up this challenge.

The research described in this book, one of a series of new studies funded
by Wallace in 2019, updates that earlier research, examining the contem-
porary literature on principal preparation and development programs,
reviewing state and federal policies, and conducting empirical research on
the relationship between principal learning opportunities and school outcomes. The companion studies, *How Principals Affect Students and Schools*
(Grissom et al., 2021) and *The Role of Assistant Principals* (Goldring et al.,
2021), provide an increasingly complete picture of how school leadership
can make a difference and how it can be developed.

As we undertook this work, we were impressed by the strength of the
findings: that programs that offer preparation in key areas such as leading
instruction, developing people, managing change, and meeting the needs
of diverse learners, and those that engage in applied learning and coaching
consistently make a difference in principals' knowledge and skills. We were
also impressed by the changes that have occurred in the field over the last
15 years, including the greater consciousness in many state capitols and local
districts of the importance of investing in principals' knowledge and skills
and the greater knowledge in many programs of how to do so effectively. It
appears that research has actually made a noticeable difference in disseminat-
ing knowledge in actionable ways.

At the same time, we were struck by how uneven this progress has been
across communities, as principals in schools serving more affluent communities continue, on average, to have more access to professional learning

than those in lower-income communities, and those in states that have been disinvesting in education have lost ground in supporting principal learning, while others have strengthened their ability to meet school leaders' learning needs.

Mostly we were struck by how eager principals are for the knowledge that will allow them to be effective and how important it is to continue to iterate on this research, policy, and practice agenda until the advantages experienced by professionals who are well-supported and students in schools that are well-led are available to all.

ACKNOWLEDGMENTS

The authors thank their Learning Policy Institute (LPI) colleagues and former colleagues for their support and contributions to this research: Seher Ahmad, Cristina Alvarez, William Berry, Jee Young Bhan, Kathryn Bradley, Laura Hernández, Iris Hinh, Ashley Jones, Sharin Park, Anne Podolsky, Darian Rice, Caitlin Scott, Tina Trujillo, and Darion Wallace. We thank Anna Egalite, Ellen Goldring, Jason Grissom, Mariesa Herrmann, Constance Lindsay, and Mollie Rubin, who were simultaneously working on related syntheses, for their colleagueship, insights, and feedback.

We thank our colleagues at the National Association of Elementary School Principals and National Association of Secondary School Principals for their partnership in administering surveys to their members. This research benefited from the insights and expertise of two external reviewers: Kenneth Leithwood, Professor Emeritus, University of Toronto, Ontario Institute for Studies in Education; and Margaret Terry Orr, Professor, Fordham University. We thank them for the care and attention they gave the book. Without their generosity of time and spirit, this work would not have been possible.

The vignettes provided in Chapters 2 and 3 of this book were adapted from *Preparing Leaders for Deeper Learning* (Wechsler & Wojcikiewicz, 2023). We thank Harvard Education Press and the authors for sharing these poignant examples of strong principal development practices.

This research was supported both financially and intellectually by The Wallace Foundation. We thank our colleagues in the foundation for their advice and counsel along the way, as well as their longstanding commitment to this work. We are grateful to Bronwyn Bevan, Lucas Held, Pam Mendels, Will Miller, Jody Spiro, and Elizabeth Ty Wilde.

Core operating support for the Learning Policy Institute is provided by the Heising-Simons Foundation, William and Flora Hewlett Foundation, Raikes Foundation, Sandler Foundation, and MacKenzie Scott. We are grateful to them for their generous support. The ideas voiced here are those of the authors and not those of our funders.

1
THE IMPORTANCE OF PRINCIPAL LEARNING

The importance of effective principals for students' and teachers' success has been well established. Research has shown that principals are a critical school-level factor influencing teacher practices and student outcomes, including student achievement, graduation rates, and attendance rates (Bartanen, 2020; Coelli & Green, 2012; Grissom et al., 2015, 2021; Leithwood & Louis, 2012; Leithwood et al., 2004). In fact, a recent summary of the evidence on principal effects concludes that, given the scope of principal effects across an entire school, "It is difficult to envision an investment with a higher ceiling on its potential return than a successful effort to improve principal leadership" (Grissom et al., 2021, p. 43).

Principals influence important teacher outcomes as well. A principal's ability to create positive working conditions and collaborative, supportive learning environments plays a critical role in attracting and retaining qualified teachers and developing their skills (Grissom, 2011; Grissom et al., 2021; Hughes et al., 2015). Indeed, teachers cite principal support as one of the most important factors in their decision to stay in a school or in the profession (Podolsky et al., 2016).

These positive student and teacher outcomes are associated with principals who effectively set direction; develop staff; have thoughtful, instructionally focused interactions with teachers; manage and redesign organizations; build positive school climates for students and teachers; and lead instruction (Grissom et al., 2021; Leithwood & Jantzi, 2006; Leithwood & Riehl, 2005). But what does it take to develop principals capable of building systems, supporting teachers, and leading instructional practices to realize these positive outcomes? That is the focus of this book.

DOI: 10.4324/9781003380450-1

Through a comprehensive and systematic research synthesis, we aimed to understand what features of preservice preparation and ongoing professional development programs for principals are associated with high-quality principal leadership behaviors, teacher practice and retention, and student outcomes. Using a California data set, we also examined how principal access to the features of high-quality preparation and professional development affects school outcomes. To understand the extent to which principals have access to these high-quality learning experiences, we analyzed principal surveys nationally and in two states with recent data. Finally, we reviewed a wide range of literature to understand trends in federal and state policies and their roles in shaping principal learning.

The Current Landscape for Principals

In 2007, *Preparing School Leaders for a Changing World: Lessons From Exemplary Leadership Development Programs* provided cutting-edge knowledge about effective preservice and in-service principal training (Darling-Hammond et al., 2007). It found that exemplary preservice and in-service programs shared a number of common elements, including meaningful and authentic learning opportunities that apply learning in practice; a focus on leading instruction, developing people, creating a collaborative learning organization, and managing change; mentoring or coaching, along with feedback and opportunities for reflection; and cohort or networking structures that create a professional learning community. In the case of preparation, proactive recruitment of dynamic, instructionally skilled teacher leaders was another key component. Highly effective in-service programs organized by districts created teaching and leadership pipelines that identified, developed, and recruited talent from their entry into the profession through multiple leadership roles. (See Table 1.1.)

Graduates of programs with these features, as well as their employers, teachers, and school stakeholders, reported that they were able to effectively engage in practices associated with school success, such as cultivating a shared vision and practice, leading instructional improvement, developing organizational capacity, and managing change. Graduates' perceptions of their preparation and of their readiness to succeed in the principalship were significantly more positive than those of a national random sample of principals. Principals who completed these programs were more likely than principals nationally to rate their preparation highly for having purposeful, targeted recruitment; a coherent curriculum; active, problem-based learning; a cohort structure and mentoring and advising to support candidate learning; well-designed and well-supervised internships; and strong relationships between local districts and universities. They also reported that they found their jobs as principals less stressful, and they were more committed to staying in the principalship than other principals, even though they were more likely to be in high-need schools.

TABLE 1.1 Characteristics of Exemplary Principal Learning Programs Identified in *Preparing Leaders for a Changing World*

Program Characteristic	Preservice	In-Service
Meaningful, authentic, and applied learning opportunities	Active, student-centered instruction (e.g., problem-based learning, action research, field-based projects) that integrates theory and practice into key leadership functions Close connections between coursework and clinical work, including supervised internships that allow candidates to engage in leadership responsibilities for substantial periods of time	Active learning that is grounded in key leadership practices (e.g., analysis and evaluation of classroom practice, applied learning of supervision and professional development practices, analysis of data, and development of school-improvement plans)
Curriculum focused on developing people, instruction, and the organization	A comprehensive and coherent curriculum aligned with state and professional standards A curriculum emphasizing instructional leadership, organizational development and improvement, staff development, and change-management skills, taught by professors and practitioner faculty knowledgeable in their subject areas	Learning that is organized around focused leadership tasks that support instructional leadership, the development of people and organizations, and the management of change, with hands-on opportunities to learn, practice, reflect, refine, and share progress in the context of data results for staff and students
Expert mentoring or coaching	Close supervision and mentoring during extended internships by expert principals knowledgeable in the program's philosophy and curriculum	Expert supervision and coaching from more senior leaders and from peers during induction and throughout the career continuum, with training and support for mentors and coaches to enable common practices
Program structures that support collegial learning	A cohort structure used to nurture collegial teams for planning and reflection	Collegial learning networks (e.g., principal networks, study groups, mentoring, and peer coaching)

(Continued)

TABLE 1.1 (Continued)

Program Characteristic	Preservice	In-Service
Proactive recruitment	Partnerships with districts that structure shared efforts for recruitment, curriculum design, and practicum learning opportunities Targeted recruitment and selection to seek out expert teachers with leadership potential Development of pipelines, funding, and time allocations to make engagement of dynamic educators in high-quality programs possible and affordable	Development of pipelines that allow for ongoing advancement through leadership ranks, coupled with strong professional learning opportunities that are freely available

Source: Adapted from Darling-Hammond et al. (2007).

Furthermore, because the programs were proactive about recruitment, the graduates of the exemplary programs were more likely to be women and people of color. They also were more likely to have had experience as instructional coaches and mentors and thus were able to build on their instructional knowledge and skills. Partnerships between the programs and districts allowed for joint recruitment and internships under the wing of expert principals.

Related research found that principals who participated in one of these exemplary leadership-preparation programs were significantly more likely than a random group of comparison principals to report that they learned about and engaged in effective leadership practices. Frequent use of those practices was positively associated with school-improvement progress and a climate of school effectiveness. The more principals experienced high-quality program features and internships, the more they used effective practices and engaged in successful school-improvement efforts. These positive relationships between the quality of preparation and leadership outcomes persisted after taking principals' prior leadership experiences and school characteristics into account (Orr & Orphanos, 2011).

In addition, teachers who worked in schools led by such well-prepared principals rated their principals' leadership practices significantly more positively than did teachers in similar schools led by traditionally prepared principals with similar levels of experience. Principal leadership had further positive and significant effects on teachers' professional development, their influence on school policies, their collaboration, and their satisfaction (Orphanos & Orr, 2014).

Since the publication of *Preparing Leaders for a Changing World*, the demands of society and the economy have changed what it means to prepare students for college and careers. In addition to mastering deep content knowledge, students need to develop skills related to problem-solving, communication and collaboration, transferring knowledge to new contexts, and critical thinking (Heller et al., 2017). Developing these skills requires teachers to provide a different kind of learning experience that is rooted in an awareness of—and responsiveness to—students' sociocultural contexts, their developmental pathways, and their individual strengths and needs (Darling-Hammond & Oakes, 2019). Additionally, research on the science of learning and development has illuminated the need to address students' social and emotional development, as well as their academic development, which requires a positive school climate, individualized supports, and productive instructional strategies that include social and emotional learning (Darling-Hammond & Cook-Harvey, 2018; Darling-Hammond et al., 2020).

Together, these advancements have begun to influence how we think about school principals. Principals must be able to follow and share a vision for deeper learning to create the learning opportunities that will prepare students for college and career; address widespread inequities in opportunities to learn; ensure cultural competence to meet the needs of the country's highly diverse student population; build collaborative communities of practice to foster deeper engagement and share expertise among fellow educators; provide staff members with learning opportunities that are developmentally grounded and personalized; and take a systems perspective to school change that is responsive to specific school and district contexts. Principals need more than administrative capacity and expertise as instructional leaders. They need the ability to redesign schools and manage change; to organize adult learning; to connect to communities; and to support rigorous, relevant learning for all students (Wechsler & Wojcikiewicz, 2023).

Because of the significant role school leaders play in shaping learning environments, preparing and developing leaders for today's schools are essential drivers of change. Therefore, it is important to understand how principal development programs—both preservice and in-service—can build principals' knowledge and skills to support learning aligned with 21st-century needs. The research behind this book was designed to help build this understanding.

Multiple Perspectives to Understand Principal Learning Opportunities

In this book, we explore four issues related to principal learning: the elements of high-quality learning opportunities and their effects on principal practices and school outcomes; the influence of various aspects of principals' learning opportunities on teacher retention and student achievement; principals' access to high-quality learning; and the role of local, state, and national policies in supporting the availability of and access to high-quality principal learning. We used different methodologies to explore each of these issues:

1. **To understand the evidence regarding high-quality principal learning,** we conducted a comprehensive review of the research literature that addresses the features of preservice and in-service principal development programs and program outcomes. We approached the review systematically, specifying search terms, defining inclusion criteria, coding each study, and evaluating the rigor and quality of each study. Of the nearly 1,400 articles identified, 104 met the criteria for inclusion. (See Box 1.1.)
2. **To understand the relationship between various aspects of principals' learning opportunities and teacher and student outcomes,** we analyzed detailed surveys of principal learning opportunities linked to state administrative files containing data on teacher, student, and school characteristics and outcome data from the California Department of Education. Controlling for other factors influencing outcomes, we examined how principals' pre- and in-service learning relates to teacher retention and student learning gains in English language arts and mathematics.
3. **To understand the extent to which principals have access to high-quality learning opportunities,** we analyzed principal survey data from representative national samples of principals affiliated with the National Association of Elementary School Principals and the National Association of Secondary School Principals. We also analyzed data from statewide principal surveys from California and North Carolina. Though initially administered for other studies, these surveys provide recent large-scale data that reflect the experiences of principals in the nation and in each state, respectively, with respect to their access to preservice and in-service learning opportunities.
4. **To understand the role of federal and state policies in shaping principal learning,** we examined over 170 articles, books, chapters, and policy reports and tracked significant policy changes over time. This review illuminates the relationship between policies and the design, implementation, and outcomes of principal learning.[1]

BOX 1.1 LITERATURE SYNTHESIS METHODOLOGY

We approached the research synthesis for principal preparation and professional development using the following three steps.

1. **Define the scope of the search.** We included studies that were published between 2000 and 2021 in a peer-reviewed journal or by an organization with established peer-review processes; focused on the outcomes of professional learning opportunities; and relied on data collected in the United States that focused on k–12 public schools.
2. **Gather and screen sources.** We began the search using ProQuest Summon and Google Scholar and identified additional literature by searching the archives of research firms and organizations with a peer-review process. We initially identified 1,380 articles and screened titles and abstracts to determine if they met our criteria for inclusion. In addition to place and time of publication as defined in the scope of the search, these criteria included having a specific focus on the outcomes of professional learning and sufficient explanation of the methods. At this stage, based on our review of titles and abstracts only, we excluded 1,078 articles that clearly did not meet the criteria.

   We reviewed the full text of the remaining 302 articles to determine if all criteria were actually met. Reviewing the full article enabled us to make this determination more accurately than our initial scan of abstracts. We also reviewed the reference lists of the articles identified to confirm that we did not overlook any key studies. We added 79 articles through this process and reviewed the full text of these additional articles as well. After reviewing the full text of the articles, we identified and eliminated 270 that did not, in fact, meet our criteria. Ultimately, 104 studies met our criteria and were included in the syntheses, which included 54 studies of principal preparation and 52 studies of in-service professional development (with two studies addressing both topics).
3. **Analyze and synthesize the literature.** Research team members coded all articles that had passed the initial abstract and full-text screens, capturing the methods employed, research design, population and sample studied, program details, context, outcomes considered, and findings. We organized and synthesized the findings from the 104 studies. We considered both the main findings and ancillary findings and assessed studies for their methodological rigor.

The general theory of action guiding our analysis is depicted in Figure 1.1. We acknowledge that principals bring different knowledge, skills, and dispositions to the job, beyond those acquired in formal training. Principals bring with them their lived experiences from their own personal and cultural contexts, from the education they received as children and young adults—as well as in their teacher preparation programs—and from the close relationships they have forged, often in the professional community.

On top of this foundation, they learn in and from the job experiences they may have had as a teacher, teacher leader or coach, assistant principal, novice principal, and experienced principal. And they learn from formal professional learning experiences, which interact with all of these other experiences in widely varying ways. As Goldring et al. (2021) found, for example, the assistant principalship, which is an increasingly important pathway to the principalship, can be formally designed and supported to increase individual and team effectiveness, although there is not yet a common approach to doing this.

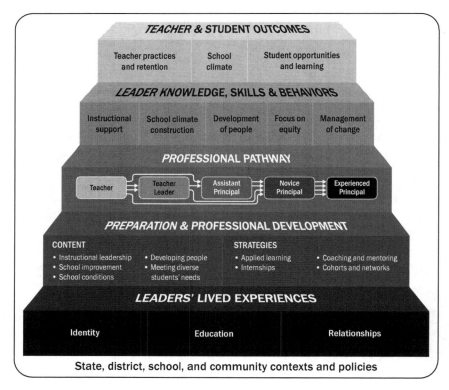

FIGURE 1.1   Theory of Action for Principal Professional Learning

In considering professional learning opportunities, we attend to both the content of the learning—what principals learn about (e.g., how to lead instruction, create collegial school environments, or evaluate teachers)—and how it is learned. The latter includes the structures that support learning, such as practicums, internships, and coursework. It also includes the pedagogies that are used, such as the extent to which opportunities support learning by designing, doing, and reflecting through the use of case studies, action research, observations in schools, and hands-on efforts to implement strategies and analyze the outcomes.

These aspects of professional learning influence leadership knowledge, skills, and dispositions—how principals lead, the school climates they establish, and their goals and actions. Leadership characteristics influence teachers—how teachers perceive and interact with others in their schools, the environments they establish in their classrooms, the learning opportunities they provide to students, and how long they choose to stay in a given school. Teachers' actions and retention ultimately influence student outcomes—how students perceive schools; their motivations and feelings of belonging; and their social, emotional, and academic development.

All of these elements are influenced by the specific policies and contexts in which they sit. For example, there are substantial differences in state licensure requirements and program-approval standards (Anderson & Reynolds, 2015; Manna, 2015). Districts and schools, too, vary considerably in their policies and practices governing principal hiring, evaluation, and professional learning; their approaches to school management; their constituents; and their local contexts.

Challenges in Studying the Influences of Principal Learning

A number of studies suggest that principal quality is associated with student learning gains (Bartanen, 2020; Coelli & Green, 2012; Grissom et al., 2015, 2021; Leithwood et al., 2004) and that specific behaviors may be particularly important in enabling these effects. The latest major research synthesis from Grissom et al. (2021) identified four classes of principal behaviors that appear to produce positive school outcomes:

1. engaging in instructionally focused interactions with teachers;
2. building a productive school climate;
3. facilitating collaboration and professional-learning communities;
4. managing personnel and resources strategically.

Other research on leadership behaviors has also pointed to the importance of *setting direction* (helping the school community develop a shared sense of purpose and vision that can motivate action); *developing people* (which may go beyond strategic management of personnel to the provision of feedback, encouragement, and high-quality professional development opportunities that develop collective efficacy in the staff); *distributing leadership and decision-making* (which can be part of collaboration but is not always emphasized); and *managing change* by using data to monitor school and student progress and to support ongoing improvement efforts (Leithwood & Louis, 2012).

How these behaviors may be developed—and how preparation or professional development may contribute to this process—is a more challenging question. In addition, research rarely addresses how these formal learning opportunities interact with principals' prior knowledge and experiences, including the extent and quality of their teaching experience and training. There is some case study evidence that shows that proactive recruitment of dynamic teachers contributes to the success of some exemplary principal preparation programs (Darling-Hammond et al., 2007). This may be because their prior experience as teachers—both the extent and quality of their teaching experience and training—influences their knowledge base about instruction as well as their capacities to mentor and help other teachers improve. For example, Goldhaber et al. (2019) found that principals who appear to be more effective in spurring student achievement also appear to have been more effective in contributing to student reading and math achievement when they were teachers. In addition, their experience before becoming a principal—perhaps as an instructional coach or assistant principal—may strongly influence their readiness for certain leadership tasks.

Not all preparation or professional development programs are alike (Hess & Kelly, 2007; Orr, 2011), and studies vary in the extent to which they describe the features of programs. On a related note, studies vary in the extent to which they describe the features of the groups to which program participants are being compared, with many failing to do so adequately. Such omissions are particularly problematic because principals' pre-program characteristics, such as their professional experiences, are also extremely important.

Clearly, there is some interaction between who is recruited to a principal preparation or professional development program, what that person understood and could do before they entered the program, and what that person is able to do as a result of the training they received. Relatively few studies provide sufficiently detailed information about candidates or participants, as well as about the content and nature of the programs they experience, to sort out which features may be associated with which outcomes.

Another factor influencing principal development is the district context. Districts vary in the ways in which they treat principals and the extent to which they support principals. These differences can undermine or augment the professional training principals have received and the extent to which principals can be effective. For example, despite evidence that principals' effectiveness is greater when they stay longer in a school (Coelli & Green, 2012) and that principal turnover negatively impacts student achievement (Béteille et al., 2012), some districts rotate principals across schools every few years (Harper, 2017). Similarly, some districts offer a coherent pipeline of preparation, mentoring, and ongoing training tightly connected to local practices, while others offer a hodgepodge of incoherent and decontextualized professional-development offerings. Thus, the effects of principals' knowledge and skills—which may be produced through preparation or professional development—can be negated or expanded by district conditions.

All of these factors should come into play when interpreting the research on principals' professional learning opportunities. Since no single research study can address all of these challenges, it is hard to draw definitive causal claims about the elements of high-quality principal learning opportunities. However, in the aggregate, the full body of research can illuminate the most promising elements.

Preview of Themes

This book brings together the existing body of research on principal learning with new research, enabling us to examine principal learning from various angles.

The chapters "Principal Preparation" and "Principal Professional Development" delve into the existing research literature on principals' initial preparation and in-service professional development, concluding that high-quality principal preparation and professional development programs are associated with positive principal, teacher, and student outcomes, ranging from principals' feelings of preparedness and their engagement in more effective practices to stronger teacher retention and improved student achievement.

The examination of the research shows that many programs have adopted the practices of exemplary leadership programs identified in *Preparing School Leaders for a Changing World*, contributing to principal and teacher effectiveness and increased student achievement. The literature also illustrates the critical importance of field-based internships and problem-based learning opportunities. The efficacy of these opportunities is enhanced when they include experienced, expert mentors or coaches who can provide support and guidance.

These chapters also explore an emerging focus on developing equity-oriented leadership. They demonstrate the potential to develop aspiring principals' knowledge and skills for meeting the needs of diverse learners.

Through applied learning opportunities (e.g., action research, field- based projects) and reflective projects (e.g., cultural autobiographies, cross-cultural interviews, analytic journals), aspiring principals can deepen their under-standing of the ways in which biases associated with race, class, language, disability, and other factors manifest in society and schools and how princi-pals can work toward more equitable opportunities and outcomes.

These findings are reinforced in the chapter "How Principal Learning Affects School Outcomes," which reports the results of a study that allowed us to examine specific attributes of principals' pre- and in-service learning opportunities in relation to teacher retention and student achievement, con-trolling for a wide range of other district, school, teacher, and student char-acteristics. The results demonstrate that the quality of preparation (based on an index of the features described earlier in this chapter) is strongly associ-ated with teacher retention, and that it is particularly important for prin-cipals to have high-quality internships in which they learn under the wing of an expert administrator for a period of time. They also show that more access to professional development in areas like instructional leadership and meeting the needs of diverse learners is significantly associated with student-learning gains in mathematics and English language arts.

In the chapter "Access to High-Quality Learning Opportunities," draw-ing on these insights into what appears to matter in principal develop-ment, we evaluate the extent to which principals experience high-quality learning opportunities across the nation and in two states: California and North Carolina. We show that most principals reported having at least mini-mal access to important content related to leading instruction, managing change, developing people, shaping a positive school culture, and meeting the needs of diverse learners. Further, access to this content has increased over time: Principals certified in the past 10 years were more likely to report access to these areas of study than earlier-certified principals. Even with these improvements, however, a minority of principals nationally reported having had access to the authentic, job-based learning opportunities that the research has identified as being important to their development. Only 46% of principals reported having had an internship during their preparation that allowed them to take on real leadership responsibilities characteristic of a high-quality internship experience, and very few in-service principals reported having access to coaching or mentoring.

We further describe how principals' access to high-quality learning opportunities varies across states and by school poverty level, reflecting dif-ferences in state policies. For example, compared to principals nationally, a greater percentage of California principals reported that they had access to preparation and professional development in nearly every important con-tent area, including areas focused on equity and teaching diverse learners, and a greater percentage reported that they had authentic, job-based learning opportunities in both pre- and in-service contexts. These opportunities were equitably available across low- and high-poverty schools. This access reflects recent changes made to state licensure and accreditation policies. At the same time, after many years of budget cuts, North Carolina principals reported having far less access to nearly every kind of professional development, and those in high-poverty schools were less likely than those in low-poverty schools to be able to access these learning opportunities.

Similarly, access to high-quality preparation varies by school poverty level nationally. Principals in low-poverty schools across the country were much more likely to report that they had learning opportunities in important areas compared to principals in high-poverty schools, and they were more likely to report that they experienced problem-based and cohort-based preparation. Likewise, principals serving high-poverty schools were less than half as likely as principals serving low-poverty schools to have access to an on-the-job mentor or coach.

Across the country, most principals reported wanting more professional development in nearly all topics, but they also reported obstacles in pursuing learning opportunities, including a lack of time and insufficient money.

The chapter "Principal Development Policy" describes how policies related to principal preparation and in-service professional development have evolved over time and concludes that policies that support high-quality principal learning programs can make a difference. In states and districts that have overhauled leadership and preparation program standards and used them as the basis for designing preparation, clinically rich learning opportunities, and assessment, evidence suggests that the quality of principal learning has improved.

Nearly, all state and local policymakers have adopted standards for principal licensing and program accreditation. These are important levers for improvement if they are infused throughout the relevant learning, supervision, and assessment systems. However, few states have adopted other high-leverage policies, such as requiring a rigorous selection process, a clinically rich internship, district–university partnerships, or a performance-based assessment for licensure. All states developed plans to bolster their efforts to support leadership development through the Every Student Succeeds Act (ESSA), using aspects of the law to strengthen preparation, reimagine on-the-job support, advance equity-focused leadership, distribute leaders more equitably, and build leadership pipelines.

Evidence from several states and districts shows that where leadership policies and implementation are strong, access to high-quality principal learning opportunities increases. In some cases—such as Chicago Public Schools' investments in new forms of principal preparation, Pennsylvania's induction program for novice principals, and six districts' engagement in the Principal

Pipeline Initiative for career-long learning—well-implemented policies have resulted in students outperforming their peers from schools led by principals who were not participating in these programs. And in states like California and Illinois, major reforms have been associated with evidence of stronger principal preparedness, practices, and retention.

The chapter "Summary and Implications" provides an overall summary of our findings and describes the current state of the research literature, suggesting ways in which it can be strengthened. Specifically, we recommend that researchers:

- broaden the scope of research to include detailed descriptions of program content and pedagogical approaches so that there is greater knowledge about what principals have the opportunity to learn and what approaches make a difference in their practices and impacts;
- account for principals' prior experiences, for program recruitment and selection criteria, and for district context so that the design and outcomes of professional learning experiences can be better interpreted;
- better define outcome measures and include a broader spectrum of outcomes associated with principal practices as they influence school conditions, to fill the large gap in the research on the relationship between principals' views of their training and changes in student achievement;
- take a longitudinal view to allow potential effects to become visible and to provide a better understanding of the mechanisms by which principals' knowledge and skills translate to their practices and their influences on staff and students;
- pay attention to how programs are implemented so that research results can be more accurately interpreted, and programs can be better designed;
- use mixed methods skillfully to deepen understanding of program processes and effects, especially those that link program features to outcomes. For example, experimental designs can be strengthened by qualitative data about the program, its implementation, and the comparison group's experiences. Case studies can combine interviews, observations, surveys, and outcome data to shed light on program offerings and how they develop principals' knowledge and skills.

The chapter then discusses implications for policy, presenting ways in which policy can support the improvement of principal learning opportunities and access to them. Specifically, we recommend that policymakers:

- develop and better use state licensing and program-approval standards to support high-quality principal preparation and development. The stronger use of licensure and program approval standards can help ensure that programs include the features of high-quality programs and help align program content with the knowledge principals need to produce positive school outcomes. Licensure and program approval standards can also require quality internships for aspiring principals and encourage applied learning opportunities, accompanied by expert coaching and mentoring for practicing principals;

• invest in a statewide infrastructure for principal professional learning. Federal funds from ESSA Titles I and II (including the 3% state set-aside for leadership development initiatives) and the American Rescue Plan Act of 2021 can be used, along with state investments, to ensure principals have access to coordinated, high-quality, and sustained professional learning. Leadership academies and paid internships or residencies can start all principals off with strong skills;

• encourage greater attention to equity both by addressing equity concerns in professional learning and by ensuring that principals who work in high-poverty schools and those with concentrations of students of color have access to high-quality preparation and professional development. This can be done by directing professional development resources to those schools or districts and underwriting high-quality preparation for prospective principals who will work in those schools;

• undertake comprehensive policy reforms at both the state and local levels to build a robust pipeline of qualified school principals and a coherent system of development. Encourage districts, through competitive grants and/or technical assistance, to launch pipeline programs that find teachers with leadership potential and carry them along a pathway to becoming a principal. Ensure novice principals receive strong mentoring and induction and veteran leaders have quality learning opportunities that contribute to coherence in practice that supports systemic change and increased student learning.

Moving forward, improved research can continue to build the field's knowledge about how to best develop high-quality principals, and enhanced policies can create a principal learning system that, as a whole, will better serve principals and, ultimately, all children.

Note

1. Detailed descriptions of the survey methodology and results are available in the online technical supplement at https://learningpolicyinstitute.org/product/developing-effective-principals.

2

PRINCIPAL PREPARATION

Introduction

New research on principal preparation programs often focuses on programs that are seeking to change long-standing features of principal preparation increasingly viewed as problematic. Historically in the United States, principal preparation has been carried out under the banner of general administrative credentialing—not necessarily geared toward the job of the principal, per se. Until the 1990s, many university programs were filled by any candidate who applied who wanted to earn that credential part time while continuing to engage in their current job, often as a teacher or counselor. The incentive for many was to earn a notch on the salary schedule rather than to become a school principal.

Courses, often taken part-time on nights and weekends, treated administrative topics like budgeting and management in the abstract, without application to real-world dilemmas of school leadership (Lashway, 1999). Clinical practice, to the extent that it was required, often took the form of projects that educators would conduct in their own schools while continuing their current jobs, rather than actual tours of duty in administrative roles under the tutelage of veteran principals. Having completed this training, many did not apply for principalships, and few felt prepared to take on the challenging role of a principal (Darling-Hammond et al., 2007; University Council for Educational Administration, 2008).

As research and observation of best practice began to define the kind of preparation that could help truly prepare aspiring school leaders, and as reforms of school designs and curricula called for a broader range of

DOI: 10.4324/9781003380450-2

skills, some innovative programs began to change their approaches (Cosner et al., 2012; Orr et al., 2010). They began to proactively recruit dynamic educators in concert with district leaders; to emphasize leading instruction and developing teachers' capacities; to place program participants in salaried positions—often with state or local funding—as administrative interns working under the wing of expert principals; and to purposefully integrate meaningful, applied coursework with clinical experiences and mentoring.

The question is, what difference have these efforts made in the preparation of principals? Equally important, what features appear to influence what principals know and can do in productive ways that translate into more support for staff and better learning for students?

In this chapter, we synthesize the results of 54 research studies that examine the features of high-quality principal preparation programs and their influence on principals' knowledge and skills, school functioning, teachers, and student outcomes.

Comprehensive Principal Preparation Programs

Many studies of principal preparation focus holistically on programs in their entirety. All of the studies that met our criteria for review focused on programs that incorporate all or many of the critical features identified in *Preparing Leaders for a Changing World* (Darling-Hammond et al., 2007). These features include close partnerships between districts and programs; proactive recruitment into the program; well-supported cohorts and/or networks for collegial learning; a coherent curriculum enacted through applied learning (e.g., internships longer than 20 weeks with a mentor, action research or inquiry projects, field-based projects); and a focus on leading instruction, developing the organization, developing people, and managing change. We refer to these programs as "comprehensive principal preparation programs."

Some programs also offer continued, aligned support during a principal's first year or two on the job. We include these programs in our review of principal preparation since that is their primary purpose, and it is how they are treated in the research. Studies of comprehensive principal preparation programs examine principals' self-reports of preparation, teachers' views about their principals' leadership, and evidence of student outcomes in the schools they are leading.

Principals' Perceptions of Their Preparation

Collectively, studies of comprehensive preparation programs have consistently found that program participants and graduates felt that the programs they attended contributed to the development of their general leadership abilities as well as to more fine-grained leadership skills, such as their ability to effectively supervise staff, diagnose and handle school problems, lead groups of teachers, conduct strategic planning, and engage in collaborative decision-making and action. In interviews and surveys, participants and graduates also reported that these programs positively influenced their sense of preparation and self-efficacy (Bartee, 2012; Beard, 2018; Braun et al., 2013; Donmoyer et al., 2012; Korach & Agans, 2011; Orphanos & Orr, 2014; White et al., 2011). In one study, a program graduate described the influence of this kind of comprehensive, cohesive program:

> For me, it was the structure of the program, the projects, the way we would read something and reflect on it and have a concentrated amount of time to apply those concepts . . . and it was through the application that you could see the big picture. The learning-by-doing had the biggest impact on me and that came from the structure of the program.
>
> *(Braun et al., 2013, p. 176)*

These benefits are highlighted further in studies that compared the outcomes of participants who attended comprehensive programs to those who did not. For example, staff at one university-based preparation program significantly redesigned the program to make it much more comprehensive. They increased hours for internship experiences; hired additional highly qualified faculty members; developed and implemented assessments to measure participants' mastery of skills and knowledge; aligned curriculum with state standards and Educational Leadership Constituent Council standards to create curriculum coherence; and emphasized a focus on leading school-improvement efforts. A study compared candidates' ratings of the original program to the restructured comprehensive program. In surveys, graduates of the restructured program rated five learning outcomes significantly higher than graduates of the earlier program: (1) learning to lead for vision building, (2) learning to lead learning for students and teachers, (3) learning to lead organizational learning, (4) learning management and operations, and (5) learning to lead parent and community involvement. Ratings remained the same for the program features that had not changed: analyzing budgets and reallocating resources to achieve critical objectives (Ballenger et al., 2009).

Another study analyzed program features in 17 leadership preparation programs in relation to graduates' ratings on a common survey of what they learned in their programs. The study found that the more programs were coherently organized around instructional leadership and provided a challenging, fieldwork-rich experience, the more positively their graduates rated their learning across five leadership domains: (1) vision and ethics, (2) learning, (3) organizational learning, (4) management and operations, and (5) parent and community engagement. Candidates in these more coherent, fieldwork-based programs were also more positive about the principalship as a career (Orr, 2011).

Teachers' Perceptions of Their Principals' Leadership

Some studies included data from staff in principals' schools in addition to the principals' self- reports. One study looked at a very intensive comprehensive program in a large urban district that included targeted recruitment and rigorous selection processes, a cohort-based structure, an internship with one-on-one mentoring, and continued mentoring after program completion. Graduates who became principals in low-income elementary schools reported that they felt well prepared as instructional leaders, armed with the ability to analyze data to guide their school improvement efforts. They and their staff, who were also surveyed and interviewed, reported that the principals had successfully created a collaborative leadership model, another target of the program (Donmoyer et al., 2012).

A larger-scale survey found that teachers in the schools of principals who had graduated from the exemplary leadership programs that were part of the initial Stanford Leadership Study (Darling-Hammond et al., 2007) held significantly more positive views of their principals' leadership practices than did teachers in the schools of a nationally representative sample of elementary school principals (Orphanos & Orr, 2014). Furthermore, teachers who had more positive perceptions of their principals' leadership also felt they experienced stronger teacher collaboration and were more satisfied with their jobs.

Student Outcomes

Linking principal preparation to student achievement trends is challenging for several reasons:

- Few studies are of sufficient duration to enable changes made by a principal to take hold in a school and significantly change test scores.
- Few studies include adequate controls, which safeguard against factors other than the preparation known to influence outcomes.
- Few studies have appropriate comparison groups needed to draw apples-to-apples comparisons.
- Few studies have been able to control for important differences among principals and schools.

For these reasons, the findings of all of these studies require careful interpretation.

One large-scale study examined the long-term outcomes of a restructured program at the University of Illinois at Chicago (UIC) designed specifically to prepare principals for low-income, urban schools (Cosner et al., 2012, 2015). Program faculty replaced a traditional master's-level principal preparation program with a doctoral program that featured selective recruitment; a cohort structure; aligned coursework emphasizing equity-driven, instructionally focused urban school leadership; a full-time yearlong residency under the guidance of an expert principal (often a graduate of the same program); leadership coaching; induction; and a close district partnership. For each school run by a UIC graduate, researchers compared the combined grade 3–8 reading and math gains to the district combined grade 3–8 gains and the state's average student-growth gains. They also compared each school's gains to the district average gains for student attendance rates, freshman on-track rates, high school graduation rates, and reductions in high school dropout rates. Although the study did not control for different school characteristics, it is worth noting that UIC graduates disproportionately worked in high-poverty schools.

Researchers found that, over 11 years, 72% of elementary schools led by program graduates and 60% of secondary schools led by program graduates exceeded the state's average student-growth gains; these differences emerging by the end of principals' first years in this role. Elementary and secondary schools led by UIC graduates also outperformed district averages for student attendance rates. Secondary schools led by UIC graduates outperformed district averages for freshman on-track rates, high school graduation rates, and reductions in annual dropout rates. Additionally, of the 96 participants in the first eight cohorts who completed the residency, 65 became urban school principals within four years, nearly all in high-need schools, and 30 became district administrators or assistant principals (Cosner et al., 2012). Nearly all (90%) program participants passed the district's principal eligibility test on their first attempt, in contrast to the 40% pass rate of non-UIC participants.

Although somewhat shorter in duration, the New Leaders Aspiring Principals Preparation program—a national program that operates across multiple schools and districts—includes selective recruitment and admissions; a cohort structure; coursework on data-driven decision- making, cultural competence, instruction, and organizational culture; a yearlong residency with a mentor principal; problem-based learning; and two years of mentoring after participants become principals. A study in ten districts found, on average, larger achievement gains among students who attended schools led by New Leaders principals than comparable students who attended schools led by non-New Leaders principals in the same districts (Gates et al., 2014). However, the magnitudes of change in achievement varied substantially across districts. Four districts had more positive outcomes among students who attended schools led by New Leaders principals than those who attended schools led by principals from other programs on at least one measure. Four other districts had less positive outcomes on at least one measure. In the other two districts studied, Chicago Public Schools and New York City Public Schools, the differences in achievement were small and insignificant; however, both of these districts have other principal preparation programs similar to New Leaders, so comparing principals from the two groups was unlikely to find substantial differences.

The researchers found that achievement gains in reading and mathematics were associated with more favorable school conditions reported on principal surveys. Gains in reading were associated with higher ratings of teacher capacity; gains in math were associated with time spent on instructional leadership as well as more favorable ratings of strategies and actions taken by the district or charter management organization. These findings suggest that along with their preparation, supports for schools and principals make a difference in student outcomes.

One of the other programs operating in New York City is the city's Aspiring Principals Program (APP). The APP is characterized by a three-phase selective admissions process; a six-week summer intensive session grounded in practical, problem-based learning and aligned with the district's goals, policies, and objectives; a ten-month school residency with a mentor principal; and a transitional planning summer. The program is designed to develop aspiring principals' knowledge and behaviors in nine areas: (1) personal behavior, (2) resilience, (3) communication and the context of learning, (4) student performance, (5) situational problem-solving, (6) learning, (7) supervision, (8) management, and (9) technology.

Using administrative data sets that allowed controls for school and principal characteristics, two studies of the program (Clark et al., 2009; Corcoran et al., 2012) found little average difference in outcomes for the schools of APP principals compared to those of new principals prepared elsewhere. This finding is not surprising, however, since there is a relatively high likelihood that the comparison principals also attended comprehensive preparation programs after the state overhauled requirements several years ago to create a more common curriculum and more clinical training. However, both studies also found that APP principals tended to work in lower-performing schools that were exhibiting steeper downward trends in student achievement prior to the principal transition than the comparison schools. They both also found that, over time, the schools with APP-trained principals showed stronger improvements than the other schools.

The Principal Residency Network program in Rhode Island is a university-district partnership with rigorous entrance requirements that offers financial support, standards-based content, a coherent and relevant curriculum, a focus on equity and school reform, a high-quality internship, problem-based learning, mentoring or coaching, a cohort, and performance assessments. Participants felt the program had a great impact on their abilities to lead change and to be equity-oriented leaders (Braun et al., 2013). Researchers compared changes in school-level student achievement in English language arts and mathematics for program graduates who had been a principal or instructional leader (e.g., director of curriculum) for at least the three-year period between 2008 and 2011, disaggregated by school level and location, to that of schools serving similar students. The descriptive study found that program graduates' schools showed more growth than comparison schools in English language arts for urban ring elementary schools and urban middle schools and showed greater growth than comparison schools in math for suburban elementary schools, suburban middle schools, and urban middle schools.

A study of graduates of five comprehensive preparation programs conducted by the American Institutes for Research (George W. Bush Institute & American Institutes for Research, 2016) found that graduates of the selected programs generally had positive perceptions of their coursework and practicum experiences, but they had mixed perceptions of district supports and ongoing program supports after graduation. The programs included many of the components identified as best practices: alignment with research-based competencies; partnerships with school districts; experiential learning, including problem-based learning and internships; rigorous recruitment and selection; and on-the-job support for at least one year after graduation. Within a relatively short period of time after hiring (one to four years, depending on the cohort), there was little evidence that student achievement gains in schools led by new principals from the selected programs were better or worse than in similar schools led by new principals of other programs. However, as with the previous studies described, this research lacked information about the comparison programs. Further, the study could not control for prior teaching and administrative experience of the new principals. In fact, a key study finding was that both the districts and the preparation programs lacked high-quality data on principal characteristics and placements.

In Chapter 4, we describe a study conducted by our team that allowed for better-controlled analyses with detailed information about principals' preparation and professional development experiences and extensive controls for student, teacher, principal, and school characteristics. This study found significant associations between high-quality preparation for principals and both teacher retention rates and student achievement in their schools (Campoli & Darling-Hammond, 2022). The quality of internships in preparation programs was found to be an especially significant element in predicting both teacher retention rates and student achievement gains. As we describe below, this feature has proved critically important in many studies.

Specific Features of High-Quality Principal Preparation Programs

As described above, the studies that examined comprehensive preparation programs found positive outcomes related to principals' self-perceived development of leadership knowledge and the perception of their leadership by teachers and other staff. Several studies also found positive associations of such programs with student outcomes, although these were often not measured with sophisticated controls for the differences in students and school features.

Quite often, principals underscored the importance of how their programs integrated applied learning into intensive and extensive clinical experiences. The survey responses from principals who graduated from the five programs studied by the American Institutes for Research (George W. Bush Institute & American Institutes for Research, 2016) are common. They listed the following program features as important to principals' preparation:

- internship or residency;
- mentoring or coaching;
- focus on instructional leadership;
- reflections on the realities of the job of principal;
- cohort model and networking;
- role-playing and simulation exercises.

Other research that focused on specific program features confirmed the particularly important role of internships and applied learning opportunities tied to the realities of the principalship.

Internships

Recent research has consistently found that graduates of programs with strong internship components were more likely than graduates of programs without internships to report being knowledgeable (Hafner et al., 2012), committed (Orr & Barber, 2006), better prepared (Orr & Barber, 2006), efficacious (Versland, 2016), and able to advance in their careers (Hafner et al., 2012; Orr & Barber, 2006). For example, principals in the Los Angeles

Principal Residency Network program, which requires working at a school site with authentic engagement in leadership activities and support from a coach, all linked to content-specific courses, were significantly more likely to be satisfied with their program and to report being knowledgeable in their field than those from a nearby traditional preparation program that required considerably fewer hours in schools (only 185 hours of fieldwork over five quarters of study, as contrasted with the more than 1,000 hours typical of a full-year residency) (Hafner et al., 2012). The University of Illinois Chicago, which requires a full-year, full-time residency, integrates support from on-site principal mentors and university-based coaches, offering a coherent and coordinated structure to enhance professional learning (see Box 2.1).

BOX 2.1   THE POWER OF COORDINATED SUPPORT

At the heart of the leadership preparation program at the University of Illinois Chicago (UIC) is a full-time, year-long residency supported by a mentor principal and university coach. To create powerful learning opportunities during the residency, UIC has developed a routine—the triad meeting—that formally brings together the aspiring principal candidate, the mentor principal, and the UIC coach. At the monthly triad meeting, facilitated by the candidate, the three discuss the candidate's leadership development, plan strategies for further developing the candidate's skills, use data to assess the candidate's progress since the previous triad meeting, and develop plans of action for further development.

At one such meeting, UIC candidate Didi Swartz was joined by her mentor principal, Nicole (Nikki) Milberg, and Paul Zavitovsky, a UIC instructor and Swartz's leadership coach. Swartz was completing her residency at the school where she had worked since the previous summer as a "participant principal." With everyone seated, Swartz passed around copies of the agenda she had prepared. It read, "Strengths, opportunities, reflections: Multi-Tiered Systems of Support structures and processes, social-emotional supports, parent engagement, and coaching."

Swartz started the discussion with a description of her work over the course of the year in leading the school's overhaul of its multi-tiered systems of supports, a comprehensive instruction and intervention framework to help ensure that every student, regardless of need, has the support he or she requires to be successful. Reflecting on her work, Swartz shared, "The takeaway product is a handbook that still needs some refinement, but it outlines new processes for next year. I feel proud that that is something we developed as a team."

"Do you think there are ways you could have done it that were more in-clusive, so you are not doing so much of the lifting?" Milberg probed Swartz.

The conversation then shifted to unpacking the development of the hand-book and the leadership practices Swartz incorporated: Did teachers feel en-gaged with the process? Did Swartz do enough to actively cultivate upfront teacher buy-in? What are the pros and cons of possibly having slowed the process down to ensure greater levels of collaboration? What levels of sup-port and facilitation did Swartz need to provide to ensure that the process was teacher-driven, yet focused on the priority of the assignment? Each topic was considered in turn as Swartz, with the help of the others, engaged in a guided self-reflection.

At another point in the hour-and-a-half triad meeting, Swartz dove into her reflections on a partnership program she designed with a local high school to offer mentoring and positive behavioral examples for a group of 8th grade boys struggling with academics and social-emotional issues. She asserted, "The planning this year was, just logistically and due to timing, between myself and the [high school] students. . . . I think we need to find better ways for [the middle grades teacher] to plan with them so that they can take better leadership within the sessions with the students." At another point Swartz pondered the frequency of interaction—twice a week for 45 minutes—and whether it's enough to impact students. Seeking to affirm and push Swartz's thinking, Zavitovsky asked about evidence of effectiveness, "Is there one kid that comes to mind? What [does] that one kid's story sound like?" Swartz brightened as she related the positive changes she'd seen one 8th grade boy make over the course of the semester, while Milberg contrib-uted additional background details about the student.

The ensuing dialogue also prompted timely consideration of Swartz's future work to support her students' social-emotional development. Her residency was nearing its end, but she had not yet secured an administrative placement for the following year. The triad considered the range of possibili-ties of where Swartz may find herself next year and what she can do to have a positive impact for her future students. Zavitkovsky began by posing a ques-tion about social-emotional supports, "What are your thoughts about some kind of scalability? If next year, the kinds of behaviors that are relatively more isolated here became more normative, . . . what would you do?" Swartz paused, then proposed a few possibilities. Zavitkovsky and Milberg each offered feedback on the possibilities while Swartz hurriedly captured their feedback in the margins of her agenda, the page quickly filling with insights.

The meeting concluded with a frank discussion of Swartz's next career steps. "I'm still torn about whether it would be beneficial to be in an assistant principal role where I can develop understanding" or pursue a principalship,

Swartz admitted. Unlike many of her peers, prior to enrolling at UIC, Swartz was working at the district office and was several years removed from the classroom. Hearing Swartz's back and forth, the others in the meeting offered no uncertain advice. "Assistant principal can be great as long as the principal is great. . . . Everything ties to that kind of professional marriage." Nodding in agreement, Milberg encouragingly added, "You should be at a school where you have a co-leadership position, otherwise you will not be happy." Swartz smiled in agreement.

Source: Wechsler, M. E. & Wojcikiewicz, S. K. (2023). *Preparing leaders for deeper learning*. Harvard Education Press.

Orr and Barber (2006) surveyed graduates from two university-district partnership programs with internships and one conventional program. Graduates of the partnership programs were more likely to rate the effectiveness of their program structures highly. Furthermore, the researchers found that the scope and quality of the internship was the most influential program element on the three outcomes studied: (1) a commitment to educational leadership, (2) a perceived sense of preparedness for the principalship, and (3) an ability to obtain administrative positions shortly after completing the program. Versland (2016) surveyed all principals in Montana to identify preparation program elements that contributed most to self-efficacy. She found that every highly efficacious principal in the study had a long-term internship with opportunities to operationalize the concepts learned in coursework and to lead teachers in school improvement strategies. Many studies examining principals' views of their programs have found they felt well prepared for the principalship due to their internships (Bartee, 2012; Perez et al., 2011; Stevenson & Cooner, 2011; Thessin & Clayton, 2013). For example, 100% of graduates of the redesigned Principal Corps at the University of Mississippi, which requires a full-year internship under the tutelage of a mentor principal, agreed that the internship prepared them well for administrative practice; 90% of them strongly agreed (Bartee, 2012).

Other studies have found a strong relationship between the internship and the development of principals' specific skills, such as their ability to establish a vision for learning and lead instruction (McCotter et al., 2016; Perez et al., 2011; Saleh et al., 2006); to understand and use data to motivate and monitor change (Perez et al., 2011); to shape a positive school climate by working collaboratively and bringing stakeholders together (Perez et al., 2011; Saleh et al., 2006); and to develop teachers by supporting their individual needs and expanding capacity through distributed leadership

(McCotter et al., 2016; Perez et al., 2011). Internships also appeared to influence aspiring principals' understanding of the principalship role (Perez et al., 2011) and the transformation of their identities from teacher to principal (Simmons et al., 2007).

The way the internship achieves these outcomes is illuminated by one study of a master's degree preparation program with a required 18-month field experience (Perez et al., 2011). During the field experience, all participants were required to create an advisory committee of teachers, other administrators, and support staff to review data; construct a vision for improvement; and develop strategies for instructional improvement, student engagement, professional development, and parent involvement. Participants also engaged in management practices, such as analyzing master schedules and teacher assignments, reviewing the collective bargaining agreement, reviewing district policies and procedures, and modifying budgets to ensure their proposed strategies were appropriately aligned with each. In interviews, a majority of candidates reported that, due to the field experience, they came to see the work of school leadership as complex and saw how various aspects of leadership were interrelated; they developed deeper recognition of the leader's role in fostering trust and relationships, encouraging collaboration, and building leadership capacity within schools; they conceptualized data as powerful evidence to stimulate the urgency for change; they articulated greater confidence as leaders and change agents; and they demonstrated increased understanding of, and ability to enact, specific leadership practices aimed at improving students' learning. One program participant described the influence of fieldwork activities related to setting a school vision:

> Now I have an understanding of what it means to create and try to live by a vision, so that it guides any decisions that I make. That's a whole new understanding of what it means to be an instructional leader.
> *(Perez et al., 2011, p. 239)*

Another described how her internship changed her perceptions of the leaders' role:

> I used to think that the core work was about managing people and a school. Now I think it's about ensuring that there is a transformation, and, in order to do that, [principals] have to make sure that everyone is learning and engaged in the transformation.
> *(Perez et al., 2011, p. 241)*

Studies that have investigated the relationship between clinical training and leadership development at a state or national level have consistently concluded that the internship is important to principals' development (Dodson, 2014, 2015; Gümüş, 2015; Militello et al., 2009; Ni et al., 2019). In a national survey of recent graduates of leadership preparation programs, Ni et al. (2019) found that graduates' internship experiences were significantly associated with their self-reports of "overall leadership learning," which includes instructional leadership, strategic leadership, ethics and professional norms, operations and management, supportive and equitable learning environments, family and community engagement, and professional and organizational culture. In one study, an intern reported on his preparedness:

> I began to think about all the responsibilities that a principal has. The decisions that have to be made, and the composure you must maintain. As I complete my internship and begin to apply for jobs, I know I am ready to accept this responsibility.
>
> *(Stevenson & Cooner, 2011, p. 293)*

In combination, the studies found that internships are most successful in developing aspiring principals' knowledge and skills when they provide opportunities for the intern to operationalize concepts learned in coursework and engage in real context-based leadership activities. In one study, a program graduate described the range of leadership activities she engaged in as an intern:

> I did a lot of hiring, a lot of the interview processing. I finished up the school improvement plan and created a more detailed plan—we had just gone through . . . accreditation and so I took that data and I came up with a plan of, okay, this is where we're weak. How can we improve on this? I organized the freshman transition program. I started the summer school online program, which I had—I wrote a grant and used that grant money to provide transportation. . . . I did a lot of memo writing and organizing for the upcoming school year. I planned a leadership team retreat.
>
> *(Thessin & Clayton, 2013, p. 802)*

Elements of successful clinical training include giving participants real opportunities to lead (Lochmiller & Chesnut, 2017; Thessin & Clayton, 2013; Versland, 2016); giving them exposure to new schools and areas of administrative work responsibilities (Lochmiller & Chesnut, 2017; Thessin & Clayton, 2013); and having mentors who are in the same building, share priorities, have trust, and are well matched (Clayton et al., 2013; Hines, 2007; Thessin & Clayton, 2013). Time is also an important aspect of clinical experiences—both time during the day for aspiring principals to work with their mentors (Lochmiller & Chesnut, 2017) and time for internships to be of sufficient length (Huang et al., 2012).

Applied Learning Opportunities

The research also consistently found that applied learning opportunities are important for principals' knowledge and skills, including their ability to analyze data, their ability to develop staff, their knowledge of discrete content, and their ability to motivate teachers and engage in effective teacher development (Batagiannis, 2011; Borden et al., 2012; Brody et al., 2010; Casey et al., 2013; Copland, 2000; Gilbert, 2017; Korach, 2011; Ovando, 2005; Sappington et al., 2010). Applied learning includes problem-based instructional approaches such as action research or inquiry projects; field-based projects in which program participants apply ideas from coursework to experiences in schools; and case studies addressing specific leadership problems, among other related activities. Active learning experiences provide opportunities for aspiring principals to practice difficult tasks in a safe setting (Friedland, 2005; Versland, 2016).

One preparation program required principal candidates to thoroughly describe and critically analyze all of the professional development activities in their schools during the preceding two years, integrating scholarly literature and identifying needed improvements in their schools (Sappington et al., 2010). Investigating the participants' final projects, the researchers concluded that most participants learned to be critical thinkers about professional development as they examined the professional development policies and practices in their schools. A majority of participants provided rich data about their schools, exhibited a clear understanding of the literature, and had important insights into the problems their schools faced regarding professional development. Furthermore, participants successfully developed appropriate recommendations for improving the professional development programs. Another preparation program required its participants to plan and present professional development sessions for preservice teachers (Casey et al., 2013). Program graduates reported in surveys that they continued to use the skills developed in this applied learning activity in their later work as principals. The program graduates also reported that the project increased their confidence in delivering effective professional development, heightened their leadership skills and abilities, and developed their collaboration skills.

In another case, an action-research project required program participants to conduct classroom observations, prepare and deliver written feedback to the teachers they had observed, and then reflect on the experience. In a questionnaire, participants reported that they learned how to conduct effective classroom observations, provide useful feedback to teachers, and provide ongoing support and resources to develop teachers' skills (Ovando, 2005). One participant described the depth of her learning in this way:

> I learned the importance of following up with a discussion about the walk-through, especially with new teachers or teachers with whom you are concerned. I learned that I should concentrate on the strengths of the teacher and be careful of how you address the areas in which the teacher might need further professional development. I learned that in order for the teacher to really receive and act on feedback given, the way in which you give that feedback is so very important. . . . I learned that being specific as to what was observed is critical and [that] in delivering the message it is a good idea to do it in person. . . . I learned that it is important to use the proper observation format. I also learned that when delivering feedback, you should be [as] specific as possible.
>
> *(Ovando, 2005, p. 178)*

In an urban school-university partnership, candidates had to complete five school-based projects in a host school, including (1) conducting an organizational diagnosis by analyzing student achievement and cultural data; (2) creating a personalized instructional leadership project; (3) engaging parents and communities as school partners; (4) conducting a student services project in which they identified student needs and evaluated instructional practices; and (5) identifying teacher-development and school-management needs and planning and executing leadership actions to promote school improvement. According to teachers in the host school, the graduates learned to challenge teachers' thinking, improve teacher practice, and expect results. Further, they knew and practiced behavioral strategies related to changing school culture (Korach, 2011). One participant described the benefits of the projects:

> On the whole, it was a wonderful opportunity to put into practice some of what we have been learning in class—we were able to observe an effort to put Understanding by Design and inclusion into practice as well as to use some of our newfound leadership skills to observe and assess teachers in this new charter school. I think we are all feeling that we are being transformed from teachers to administrators.
>
> *(Brody et al., 2010, p. 632)*

The Educational Leadership Program for Aspiring Principals at the University of Pennsylvania required daylong visits to schools, during which teams of aspiring principals visited classrooms to observe instruction, reviewed curriculum, and interviewed teachers and students. The teams prepared an oral report that they presented to the school's principal and faculty. In their study of the focused observations, Brody et al. (2010) found that, as a result of engaging in these school- based activities, aspiring principals conceptualized leadership as a complex process of critical inquiry. They also learned to engage themselves and others in implementing an instructional vision, shape effective communication that promotes individual and collective growth, embrace critical inquiry, and understand the complexity of organizational change (Brody et al., 2010).

Similarly, in the tightly aligned leadership-development pipeline programs in Long Beach Unified School District, aspiring principals and teacher leaders—many of whom are on a path that will lead to the principalship— participate in many of the instructional leadership activities in which the district regularly engages its leaders (Wechsler & Wojcikiewicz, 2023). (See Box 2.2.)

BOX 2.2 LEARNING TO LEAD THROUGH COLLABORATIVE INQUIRY VISITS

In the Long Beach Unified School District in California, aspiring principals in the district's principal pipeline learn to lead, in part, by participating in routine district leadership practices. One such practice is the Collaborative Inquiry Visit (CIV). These daylong visits bring district leaders, school leaders, and teachers into the classrooms of their peers at a hosting school site to support school improvement with a focus on teaching and learning. Aspiring principals shadow their mentors on CIV days to gain a firsthand experience of the process from the leadership perspective. During the visits, pipeline program participants observe multiple classrooms and share in conversations about the quality of teaching and learning in the school alongside teachers and school leaders from across the district. Participants also join in reflecting on the ways in which school and district leaders are working toward their goals and supporting teachers to improve school-wide instruction.

Harte Elementary School is located on a quiet residential block, just off a main road in north Long Beach. The school comprises several clusters of school buildings and portable classrooms organized around a large asphalt playground. On an overcast morning in February, CIV visitors gathered in Room 20 and chatted over bagels and coffee before the day's activities began. The visitors—principals and Instructional Leadership Team teachers from Garfield and Herrera elementary schools—sat around five tables. At the beginning of the school year, Harte, Garfield, and Herrera school leaders self-selected into a partnership based on their instructional goals for the year. Instructional

Leadership Team teachers from Harte split up to sit with their visitors. District leaders made up the final group of visitors, for a total of about 25 attendees.

The morning began with a briefing by Harte's principal, a first-year principal who transitioned to the principalship after many years as a k-12 literacy program manager in the district. She began by describing her school, including the student demographics, standardized test score trends, teaching and learning goals, and professional development offerings. Then, she introduced a theory of action for the year informed by Dylan Wiliam's *Embedded Formative Assessment* (Wiliam, 2011). The school's goal was to embed Wiliam's five strategies for formative assessment into instruction: If teachers (1) collaboratively plan lessons with clear learning goals and success criteria, (2) design activities to elicit evidence of learning, (3) provide effective feedback, (4) facilitate student to student interaction, and (5) encourage students to take ownership of their learning, then student achievement will increase and the achievement gap for ELLs will narrow.

Next, the principal previewed the lesson-plan structure that visitors would be using while observing in classrooms that day. She expressed that her goal was to build greater instructional consistency across the school: "It's important that at this school we have common pedagogy. This is a journey. Today is really a baseline for us." Over the course of the day, at least one group of CIV observers would visit each classroom, provide baseline data, and support Harte's principal in guiding the faculty in a conversation to improve practice. At the end of the briefing, groups of observers made their way to classrooms. Each group spent about ten minutes in each classroom, noting how the teacher used formative assessment strategies.

After visiting several classrooms, observers concluded that most teachers were attempting to implement the deeper learning practices reflected in the school's goal, with varying levels of success. In an exemplary lower-grade classroom, students were actively engaged and directing their own learning in a math lesson. Even before entering the classroom, observers noticed the chatter of productive conversation filling the hallway outside. Students were sitting on the rug in groups of four to six. Each group sat around a hula hoop, and at the center of each hula hoop was a bucket of objects—cups, water bottles, toys, and classroom supplies. Students worked with a partner to measure the height of objects of their choice using cubes as a standard unit of measurement. Their learning was self-directed; they chose which objects they wanted to measure, stayed engaged in the activity, and had active conversations with their partners to explain their thinking, correct misconceptions, and decide when they were ready to move on. The teacher traveled from group to group observing conversations and offering guidance. The student work displayed on the classroom walls revealed that this activity was part of a math unit on measurement and units. One set of posters, for example, featured collages of fish of different sizes. Students measured them using different types of objects as different units of measurement.

Over the course of the morning, the CIV observers continued to observe classroom after classroom. While most classrooms demonstrated at least some of the principles of high-quality, deeper-learning instructional practices that incorporate formative assessment strategies, it was clear that as a school there was still progress to be made. After observing one class, for example, Harte's principal noted that "the [teacher's] feedback was about how to do the task, not about what they were learning." Most of the teacher's comments were about where students should be sitting or which boxes they should be filling out in a worksheet, rather than on guiding students toward meaningful learning goals. While the students in that class were sitting together in groups, most worked silently on their own.

By 10:30, the five observation groups had each been in five different classrooms, reaching each of the school's 25 classrooms. Back in Room 20, the five observation groups identified patterns they saw over the course of the morning, and Harte's principal led a discussion on "stars and wishes," or what they saw that positively reflected the school's theory of action and what staff might continue working on. Observers noted that there was evidence of teacher collaboration and of students taking ownership of their learning. A common theme that arose in the conversations between classroom visits, for example, had to do with distinguishing between group work and collaborative and productive learning communities. During the debriefing conversation in the afternoon, the principal noted that in some classrooms, students were "working *in* groups, not *as* groups." While several teachers organized students into groups, few classes had students working together as productively as the primary students measuring with cubes. In a few cases, the students could have just as easily completed the assignment on their own, or it was evident that they had not practiced collaboration norms that would have made their work together productive. The purpose of the visit, however, was not meant to be evaluative, but instead to identify opportunities for growth and improvement. Throughout the morning, conversations about observations came back to what the principal might try after the day was over.

The CIV concluded with a conversation among just the school leaders, as teachers and other staff returned to their day's duties. The Garfield and Herrera principals shared what they had learned that they would be taking back to their school sites. Harte's principal shared some final reflections about how to structure the school's professional learning to get the greatest impact. In particular, she wondered if she should continue to lead teachers in using formative assessment strategies in isolation, or help teachers apply the strategies to a content area to make them more relevant.

By participating in the day, the aspiring leaders observed models of teaching and learning to calibrate their understanding of what strong instruction looks like. They saw several different classroom examples and benefited from a conversation about several additional classes. In addition, they engaged in the professional practice of working collaboratively with colleagues to set goals, and they heard how leaders think about using several approaches to support teachers.

Source: Wechsler, M. E., & Wojcikiewicz, S. K. (2023). *Preparing leaders for deeper learning*. Harvard Education Press.

While this kind of group engagement in authentic activities that inform decision making can be very powerful, it is not always possible in every setting around every area of decision making. Interestingly, two studies found that technology-based simulated applied learning can contribute to the development of principals' knowledge and skills when it augments other important program features, such as coursework and a clinical experience (Mann et al., 2011; Tucker & Dexter, 2011). For example, the Educational Theory Into Practice software provides virtual leadership cases that address organizational, instructional, and relational leadership, facilitating a structured approach to the decision-making process. Pre- and post-surveys demonstrated an increase in participants' self-perceived decision-making skills and more generalized self-efficacy, confidence, and certainty about the decision-making process (Tucker & Dexter, 2011).

Learning through experience can take many forms. A particularly innovative approach is the use of the performing arts to help leaders-in-training develop a whole child perspective for pursuing deeper learning and equity, as exemplified in the partnership between the University of California at Berkeley and the Alvin Ailey American Dance Theatre. (See Box 2.3.)

BOX 2.3   USING THE ARTS TO LEARN TO LEAD FOR DEEPER LEARNING AND EQUITY

The Principal Leadership Institute at the University of California Berkeley leverages the arts to teach aspiring principals the importance of whole child education and socially just leadership. The program does this by partnering with AileyCamp, a nationally acclaimed summer program founded by the Alvin Ailey American Dance Theatre. AileyCamp offers underserved youth, primarily children of color, six weeks of intensive, immersive dance instruction. Most campers have no prior dance training. The entire camp, including attire, meals, and transportation, is free. The goal of AileyCamp is to "use the power of dance to enrich and positively impact the lives of children" (Alvin Ailey American Dance Theatre).

By stepping into the shoes of the learner and engaging in an immersive, experiential dance education program, participants develop a keen understanding of the importance of a full curriculum, how social and emotional factors influence learning, and the empowerment and knowledge that students derive from deeper learning experiences. Further, participants learn by example how they can work toward social justice by creating art in response to hate.

Through multiple engagements with the camp, including a dance lesson, open house, and interviews with campers, aspiring principals deepen their understanding of how schools can use the arts to disrupt issues of access to and opportunity for the types of enrichment that AileyCamp provides. Working with AileyCamp equips future leaders with specific tools for leveraging arts curricula to help even the playing field in traditionally under-resourced communities.

On one of the early days of the AileyCamp experience, each member of the new 24-person cohort meets at the massive Zellerbach Auditorium at the University of California at Berkeley. They each stare out at the theatre, hotfoot across the stage, and deposit their bags so they can get to work. Their jokes and laughter turn to hushed, nervous whispers, then silence. David McCauley, their instructor, is a tall, lithe Black man whose graceful movements confirm his years spent in the Alvin Ailey American Dance Theatre. The purpose of AileyCamp, he stresses, is to expose historically disadvantaged middle school students to the arts, while building discipline and social-emotional learning skills. He speaks with affection of his mentor, Alvin Ailey, who was known for incorporating his dancers' moves into his choreography because, "dance comes from the people and should go back to the people." The camp, McCauley shares, features daily, positive self-talk and affirmations about "the way that you treat yourself and others." Students kick off each morning with phrases such as "I am open" and "I will not let 'can't' define my possibilities."

Today, the aspiring principals sit where Ailey campers normally do. They've gathered here as part of their work preparing to become social-justice-oriented leaders in schools that serve historically marginalized students. Today's experience will inform one of their assignments: a paper on theories of transformative teaching and learning.

Program staff believe that at the root of transformation is discomfort, and these aspiring leaders are bathing in discomfort on the stage. The lights illuminate the barefoot participants as some giggle nervously while McCauley models each dance step. Their first is a simple body roll. He tilts his head forward and rolls toward the ground, one vertebra at a time. He narrates his moves, highlighting key details, such as position and how it should feel as they roll forward. Later, he adds music to their practice.

The group soon picks up pace as they become more acquainted with McCauley's steps. He watches them while he models, constantly assessing their needs and progress. Then he stops the cohort; over half of them are struggling with a particularly challenging move. They will "just practice staying on one leg first," he states jovially. The shift elicits a chorus of relieved laughter. As they move into the multi-step iteration, McCauley repeats "off, fall on it, press, and close," a shorthand for the sequence, until the group is moving fluently again. They bob up-and-down and sway side-to-side as a unit, sharing a rhythm set out for them by McCauley. Before long, he's steadily increased the rigor of the sequence until the novices are doing *tendus* and *pirouettes* across the stage.

Eventually, they break from the warm-up. McCauley shares that, because today gives just a taste of AileyCamp, they will skip forward to work that takes place later in the summer: rehearsing for the final performance. He scaffolds this sequence with ease and expertise, counting each of his movements aloud, then pausing for a beat before asking the class to follow. Next, he chunks steps together, narrating the emotion behind each progression. He holds his hands above his head, eyes wide, and mimes pushing back against invisible forces, the ones that are "oppressing you and trying-to-hold-you-down." He pauses to contextualize their learning. The dance, he explains, comes from Ailey's *Revelations*. It features members of the corps in a diverse array of flesh-colored costumes, and it represents the repentance of Sunday morning. The spiritual song "I Been Buked" serves as the foundation for their movements, each pose flowing with the richness of the baritone, expressing the cascading grief that comes with each word. At this point, several cohort members stand up straight, focus more intently, and let go of the remnants of their awkward giggles. The collective demeanor shifts. They have been tasked with something meaningful, spiritual, and larger than themselves. McCauley sings the spiritual as they move, some with jaws clenched in focus, others whispering the cues under their breath.

The day concludes with two performances. In each, McCauley taps unlikely students to assume leadership roles, to stretch themselves. His humor puts them at ease and makes his unwavering high expectations more welcome. By noticing the strengths, comfort-levels, and dynamics of the collective, he surfaces the leadership capabilities that individuals may have, but may not be comfortable exhibiting on stage. When the aspiring principals perform, they melt into a shared rhythm that guides them smoothly through each step, finishing as a collective with hands held firmly toward the sky. The audience erupts in boisterous applause as the relief, joy, and sense of accomplishment wash over the principals-in-training.

Source: Wechsler, M. E., & Wojcikiewicz, S. K. (2023). *Preparing leaders for deeper learning*. Harvard Education Press.

Meeting the Needs of Diverse Learners

Over the past two decades, a new research focus related to principal preparation has emerged: understanding how to best prepare principals to meet the needs of students from diverse racial, ethnic, linguistic, and cultural backgrounds. Different programs use different terminology, such as equity leadership, leadership for social justice, or culturally responsive leadership. Their efforts may include a single course or an entire program. Comparative research shows that engagement in applied learning opportunities (e.g., action research, field-based projects) and reflective projects (e.g., cultural autobiographies, cross-cultural interviews, and analytic journals) can lead to growth in aspiring principals' awareness about how to meet the needs of diverse learners.

For example, a full-time two-year master's degree program at a large flagship university in the Southeast designed a suite of experiences to develop aspiring principals' ability to engage in culturally responsive leadership. Program components included cultural autobiographies, life histories, diversity workshops, cross-cultural interviews, diversity presentations and panels, and reflective analytic journals. Brown (2005) compared two cohorts that took the Social Context course in the fall semester to two cohorts that took a School Management course in the fall. (The following spring, the course assignments were switched.) Based on pre- and post-surveys using the Cultural and Educational Issues Survey (Pettus & Allain, 1999, Version B), the research confirmed improved attitudes toward issues of diversity in education for the group that took Social Context, while the group that took School Management regressed. An analysis of candidates' weekly journals also revealed that all 40 candidates in the Social Context course became conscious of practices that lead to systemic inequities and developed a sense of responsibility to change them.

Another program that was focused on developing culturally responsive leadership integrated equity theory, inquiry, fieldwork, and reflection focused on understanding oneself and others through the lens of culture through-out the program (Gordon & Ronder, 2016). Through interviews, research-ers found that end-of-program candidates generally had more sophisticated conceptions of culturally responsive leadership than new-to-the-program participants and school administrators who had not attended the program. Rather than identifying special programs for different groups of students, these graduates understood that culturally responsive leaders build relation-ships and work collaboratively with students, teachers, and parents to make the school more culturally responsive; provide professional development to teachers; and regularly communicate with parents and the community to bring them into the school. As one program participant said, for example:

> I think they [culturally responsive leaders] attempt to make a connection with the students that's on a personal note—a personal level—that may be directly related to that student's culture, trying to find a common ground and really looking at a student as an individual.
>
> *(Gordon & Ronder, 2016, p. 138)*

Research suggests that even a single course about meeting the needs of diverse learners can be linked to the development of principals' skills in this area. For example, a course on school-community relations that included a community service project related to cultural proficiency increased par-ticipants' dispositions for community connection (Keiser, 2009). Even more powerful is an approach that infuses concerns about equity into every course, as the University of Illinois, Chicago has done with its educational leadership program. (See Box 2.4.)

BOX 2.4 DEVELOPING AN UNDERSTANDING OF RACE AND JUSTICE

The University of Illinois at Chicago (UIC) has deliberately structured its cur-riculum so that all courses address how social constructs such as disability, race, ethnicity, language, gender, and social class influence teaching, learn-ing, and leadership in schools. UIC expects program graduates to be able to "demonstrate a professional-level, research-informed response" to questions like: What does it mean to say that "intelligence" is a socially constructed concept, and that the idea of intelligence as a hereditary trait is mislead-ing? How can a school staff get smarter about issues of race and ethnic-ity in constructive ways that build instead of damage social trust? What is the difference between being neutral to gender differences in students and colleagues vs. being gender sensitive vs. being gender biased? When does gender matter? How and why does economic class matter to student achievement in the U.S.? What is "leadership for social justice," and how is it consistent or inconsistent with professional standards in the school leadership field (University of Illinois at Chicago College of Education, 2016, p. 1)?

Consider Paul Zavitkovsky's course, Introduction to Practitioner Inquiry. At the beginning of one class, Zavitkovsky shared with his students that the goal of the class was to "[move] from the unconscious to conscious and making the invisible visible. . . . The hope is that we will provide you with some tools for being able to do that not only with others but with yourself." One focus of the class is for students to learn how to address the racial achievement gap that persists in Chicago Public Schools. A key aspect of this development is for participants to learn how to make the teachers and staff in their schools aware of the root causes of the gap.

Zavitkovsky first reminded the participants about the issues they learned about while reading *Racism Without Racists*, by Eduardo Bonilla-Silva, the first reading they completed in their first class, Organizational Leadership (Bonilla-Silva, 2017). The book introduced the participants to the issues of "color-blind racism," which views racial inequalities "as the product of market dynamics, naturally occurring phenomena, and blacks' imputed cultural limitations." According to the book, color-blind racism ignores how social institutions and structures oppress people of color. To demonstrate the weaknesses of color-blind racism, the book illustrates the role of broader societal structures in generating racial and socioeconomic inequities.

After reminding the class of their past learning, Zavitkovsky connected the challenges of racial inequality to participants' experiences in the schools where they have taught:

> When it comes to the discipline, punishment, and the exclusion side, I ask you to think about schools where discipline is a problem, and think about the discipline rates and exclusion rates and how those things break out by race and class. There is no mystery about how those things break out by race and class.

After that, Zavitkovsky challenged the participants to take a critical stance and reflect on conventional approaches to educating lower-income students and students of color:

> I ask you to think about race and class from the point of view: What it is that we think [students of color from low-income families] are capable of doing? To what extent is our curriculum for those particular youngsters guided by our implicit sense that we really have to deal mostly with basic

skills and the most fundamental things before we think they can deal with the most interesting things? I ask you to think about that.

Participants then broke into small groups to, as Zavitkovsky described, "[generate] some starting points for leading conversations that help [them] and others stop being unwitting parties to institutional racism and classism." A student in one group raised the challenges she has faced when trying to push her school to move from conventional supports to transformational supports for teaching and learning:

> I've seen multiple times that schools, leadership, someone will say, "just give me the silver bullet." . . . They are like, "We are drowning and we're not doing good work by our kids. We need something to fix this problem now." And I always argue that while I understand your motivation, over the long term, there's no system in your school. You're just giving someone a scripted curriculum and assessments that go with it and saying, "use this and you'll be fine." You might have the appearance of fixing the problem. But you don't. You just perpetuate the same thing. Because no one has an investment in the work and actually developing as an instructor as part of this long, drawn-out, difficult, messy, complex process.

The student's comment reflected an awareness of how instruction for students from low-income families and students of color has traditionally been more focused on developing basic skills—in part because of the pressures that have accompanied test-based accountability policies. The student recognized that making shifts in organizational culture and practice takes time and requires collaboration among teachers, staff, and leaders. These shifts also require leaders to make the negative effects of short-term solutions visible to staff so that they will invest in sustainable deeper-learning instructional strategies that promise to improve the learning of all students.

Source: Wechsler, M. E., & Wojcikiewicz, S. K. (2023). *Preparing leaders for deeper learning*. Harvard Education Press.

It is important to note, however, that backgrounds of program participants can affect how programs' efforts to teach equity-oriented leadership are taken up and used—and their results. A few studies examined the engagement in and outcomes of equity-centered programs from the perspectives of participants of different racial and ethnic backgrounds (Guerra et al., 2013; Jacobs et al., 2013; Williams et al., 2018). These studies showed that participants come into programs with different understandings and experiences with racial diversity and, therefore, experienced the programs differently.

For example, Jacobs et al. (2013) studied how participants in an educational leadership program operationalized social-justice theory during an action-research activity. They found that white participants tended to become equity-oriented through "professional cultural intuition"—their experiences in Title I schools or schools that were experiencing demographic shifts. In contrast, participants of color often drew on their "navigation capital"—their own personal experiences—in addition to professional cultural intuition. Further, while all participants recognized that building relationships with faculty, staff, and communities of color was integral to facilitating change on their school campuses, participants of color were more likely to develop relationships with parents by affirming their experiences and cultural backgrounds. Thus, the outcomes of programs are a combination of both what the programs do and whom they recruit, and the design of program strategies may need to be sensitive to the various ways in which participants can access the learning opportunities and make sense of them.

Most studies of efforts to meet the needs of diverse learners focus on students of color. We identified only one study focused on meeting the needs of LGBTQ students. Marshall and Hernandez (2013) examined two preparation courses that focused on social justice, highlighted the needs of LGBTQ students, and found that participants became more analytic and less passion-driven when discussing sexual orientation—and that they developed concern about their districts' lack of attention to sexual orientation and its negative effect on students and staff.

Principal Preparation Research: Limitations and Opportunities

In synthesizing the research on principal preparation, we found that study design, program participants, and program implementation can influence research results. Just as the programs we studied varied considerably, so did the methodologies employed to study these programs. For each study we reviewed, we were interested in understanding the details of the methodology to assess the strength of the evidence supporting the researchers' conclusions. For example, a number of the descriptive studies had small sample sizes, focusing on single cohorts or spanning short periods of time, which limited the generalizability of their findings. However, the consistency of findings across a large number of studies provides some reassurance about the overall conclusions we were able to draw.

There are fewer studies that focus on student achievement, and in many cases, their limitations influence what can be interpreted from the findings.

For example, Donmoyer et al. (2012) noted in their examination of student achievement trends that the two years covered by the study were insufficient for producing achievement gains. Further, they recognized that they did not have a sufficient sample size or a set of controls to draw valid conclusions about the mix of trends that they identified. Braun et al. (2013) faced similar limitations, noting that due to small sample sizes, the findings they present related to student achievement were descriptive only, with no tests of statistical significance.

Other studies with large samples were unable to account for the preparation of their comparison groups, such as in the study of the New York City Aspiring Principals Program (APP) conducted by Corcoran et al. (2012). Given that the state overhauled its program requirements and that program quality in New York City is relatively high, it is likely that the comparison principals also attended high-quality preparation programs. If so, the lack of difference detected does not mean the APP was ineffective. Rather, it may mean that the treatments and outcomes were not significantly different among programs.

There are other issues when comparing new principals operating in the same district context. In the study of New Leaders, Gates et al. (2014) recognized that the estimates of New Leaders' effects may be smaller because of districtwide changes that give advantages to all principals, not just New Leaders principals. Further, sites varied in terms of their concentration of New Leaders principals, access to other principal preparation, and the extent to which principals had decision-making authority, all factors influencing study outcomes. As in the study of the APP, some districts, including Chicago Public Schools and New York City Public Schools, had many non-New Leaders principals who received similar training, so principals from the two groups were unlikely to show substantial differences.

Another factor influencing the interpretation of these comparison studies was the inability of the researchers to control for differences in who was selected into the various programs. As a result, principals often had important differences from the start. For example, compared to principals coming through other routes, principals from the APP had less prior teaching experience and assistant principal experience, restricting the knowledge bases they were able to bring to their training and to the job (Corcoran et al., 2012), and this limitation can be conflated with the quality of the program itself when examining outcomes.

All of these implementation and methodology factors temper the conclusions we are able to draw about the link between principal preparation and student achievement.

Further, despite the extensive research base on the design and outcomes of principal preparation, unanswered questions remain. The field would benefit from additional research focused on what newly trained principals do in their schools, whether and how they change school culture and practices, and the links between principal preparation and teacher outcomes and a broad array of student outcomes. The research that goes deep into clinical experiences and applied learning opportunities illuminates various models and their potential outcomes. Little in-depth research exists on other program components, such as coursework, recruitment and admissions, and cohort models. The field would benefit from deep dives into each of the features of preparation programs. Research is also lacking on principal induction and how it may build on initial preparation. And the new research on meeting the needs of diverse learners needs to be expanded to include a wider range of comparisons and outcomes, as well as concerning different populations of students, such as students with disabilities or dual-language learners.

3

PRINCIPAL PROFESSIONAL DEVELOPMENT

Introduction

There are some notable similarities between the research on in-service principal professional development and principal preparation. As with the preparation programs studied, many of the in-service professional development programs studied had been newly developed or redesigned to reflect emerging knowledge about the characteristics of high-quality professional development. Like the research on principal preparation, the research on in-service professional development includes studies that examine programs in their entirety and others that focus on specific program features, such as coaching or mentoring, networks, or applied learning opportunities. In this chapter, we synthesize the findings of 52 research studies to examine how programs and their features influence principals' practices and perceptions, aspects of school functioning, and student outcomes.

Comprehensive Professional Development Programs

A number of studies of principal professional development focus on programs in their entirety. The programs studied include some or all of the features of exemplary programs identified in earlier studies (e.g., Darling-Hammond et al., 2007). We refer to these programs as "comprehensive principal development programs." Their features include content focused on leading instruction, managing change, shaping a positive school climate, and developing people; individualized, one-on-one support provided by a

DOI: 10.4324/9781003380450-3

coach or mentor; opportunities for networking with peers, often in structures like professional learning communities (PLCs); and opportunities for authentic, job-embedded, applied learning activities. These studies examine a range of outcomes, including principals' views of their knowledge and practice and the effect of principal participation on student achievement.

Principals' Views of Their Knowledge and Practice

Studies have consistently found that principals participating in comprehensive professional development programs with the features of high-quality professional learning report increases in their understanding of leadership and improvements in their leadership practices (Barnes et al., 2010; Camburn et al., 2016; Hewitt et al., 2014; Leithwood et al., 2003; Nunnery et al., 2010; Nunnery, Ross, et al., 2011; Nunnery, Yen, et al., 2011; Tingle et al., 2019).

For example, a university-district partnership in a large, urban, southwestern school district developed a program that focuses on instructional leadership, human capital, executive leadership, school culture, and strategic operations using applied learning opportunities. The cohort-based program offered a peer network and individualized mentoring. In a principal survey and interviews, program participants reported that participation positively influenced their effectiveness in leading instruction, developing people, building a positive school culture, and managing operations (Tingle et al., 2019). Another program, IMPACT V, was created through a partnership between the North Carolina Department of Education, four educator preparation programs, and 11 school districts. Principals participated in monthly leadership development institutes and monthly executive leadership coaching sessions in their schools, during which they reflected, problem-solved, and assessed progress on their leadership skills, their professional goals, and their schools' improvement action plans. Through an analysis of artifacts collected before and after program participation, researchers found that principals developed skills in creating a shared vision and in building goal consensus; building structures to enable collaboration; leading for strategic and systematic change; and modeling desired behaviors, beliefs, and values (Hewitt et al., 2014).

Principals who participated in comprehensive programs report greater gains in knowledge and skills than others who did not. The Ohio Leadership for Inclusion, Implementation, and Instructional Improvement (OLi4) program, for example, is a two-year professional development program designed to enhance school leaders' "inclusive instructional leadership" by emphasizing equity and social justice. The program consists of nine professional development sessions per year, practical school-based assignments, monthly school-based coaching, and school district engagement. Comparing survey responses of participants to those of a matched group of principals who did not participate, researchers found that program participants reported significantly higher ratings on their attitudes toward inclusive instructional leadership practices and on their practices of working with teachers on collaborative problem-solving and collaborative professional learning (Howley et al., 2019).

Another school-university partnership, the Brigham Young University Principals Academy, conducted in partnership with five school districts, illustrates how program design and implementation can make a difference in outcomes. The first cohort met for approximately 20 days over a two-year period and worked on how to implement PLCs in their schools. Due to a change in program management, the second cohort focused on refining PLCs and developing their leadership capacities, with fewer opportunities for networking and collaboration. Based on a comparison of pre- and post-Academy survey results, the first cohort of principals demonstrated growth in all measured learning outcomes (i.e., vision and mission, team collaboration, common assessments, data analysis). The growth of the first cohort of principals was corroborated in a separate study in which district supervisors reported improvements in principals' practice (Boren & Hallam, 2019). After changes to the program, the second cohort of participating principals did not demonstrate growth in learning outcomes. Through interviews with participating principals, the researchers identified challenges stemming from changes in program management and content, as well as weak support from some districts (Boren et al., 2017).

One of the largest professional development programs for principals is the National Institute of School Leadership (NISL), which has served more than 12,000 school and district leaders in at least 27 states. NISL features a cohort model embedded within participating districts; networking opportunities; online and face-to-face instruction over 12 to 15 months; applied learning experiences that result in a performance assessment; and interactive learning with self-assessments, simulations, case studies, school evaluations, and online activities. Facilitators meet with participants individually and in small groups. In some contexts, NISL also offers one-on-one mentoring to principals; in others, principals work with their already-assigned local mentors. Taking a systems approach, NISL also offers training for principal supervisors in a school-leadership coaching program so that they can leverage the NISL experience for the participating principals, creating a coherent approach at each level of the system (National Center on Education and the Economy, n.d.).

The research-based curriculum, which consists of three comprehensive courses that can be taken for university credit, is unusual in how deeply it covers leadership content. Coursework presents the knowledge base on how people learn and its implications for teaching, leadership, and design of the school organization. For example, there is a focus on the integration of social, emotional, and academic learning; content pedagogy; and culturally responsive teaching. The curriculum also emphasizes strategic systems thinking for transforming schools into learning organizations focused on effective instruction and equity. Participants apply their learning by deeply analyzing their own contexts, developing theories of action, and enacting related strategies in their schools. They are aided by facilitators who work with them individually and in small groups focused on common action-learning themes. This facilitator support continues for three to six months beyond coursework until participants present their strategies and results in a capstone project.

The RAND Corporation conducted two evaluations of NISL. One study found, via surveys and interviews, that participating principals felt that the program improved their abilities to conceptualize and lead school-improvement efforts and that they highly valued both the program content and NISL coaching. Nine in-depth case studies of schools illustrated that participants enacted the program's core concepts and processes in ways that supported staff uptake of school-improvement efforts, leading to changes in teachers' instructional practices (Wang et al., 2019).

The second study analyzed the effects of the NISL program paired with coaching (Master et al., 2020). It examined 332 middle school principals who were located in 118 school districts in three states. Half of the principals were randomly assigned to receive the NISL training and coaching; the other half had the option to receive the training three years later. The researchers found large positive effects on two practices taught by the program—having a strategic plan and personalizing student instruction—and marginally significant effects on teachers' reports of collaboration. The study also found positive outcomes related to student achievement, described in the next section.

Student Outcomes

While studies overwhelmingly found a positive relationship between comprehensive in-service professional development and principals' views of their knowledge and practice, as with principal preparation, linking principal professional development to student achievement is challenging. Studies need to be of sufficient duration, with adequate controls and an appropriate comparison group. Additionally, it is important to understand program design and implementation to be able to interpret the findings. In this section, we focus on the studies that found a clear, positive relationship between comprehensive professional development and student achievement. We turn to the studies with more complex implementation challenges in the following section.

The research reporting positive student-achievement results includes several studies of NISL. Studies in Pennsylvania (Nunnery, Yen, et al., 2011) and Massachusetts (Nunnery et al., 2010) compared student achievement in schools led by NISL-trained principals to that in schools led by principals who did not participate in NISL. The schools were matched by student performance in math and English language arts, the proportion of economically disadvantaged students, the proportion of students receiving special education services, and the proportion of students with limited English proficiency. Analyzing achievement rates in the three years following the NISL training, both studies found significantly higher rates of improvement on state tests for the schools led by NISL graduates. The Pennsylvania study found significantly larger gains in mathematics, and the Massachusetts study found significantly greater gains in both mathematics and English language arts. A follow-up study in Pennsylvania confirmed the higher rates of gain over an additional year (Nunnery, Ross, et al., 2011).

Another large-scale study focused on Pennsylvania's Inspired Leadership (PIL) Program, an induction program for novice principals that relies on NISL practices. This study found that schools with principals who participated in PIL induction showed improved student math achievement. The researchers linked the increases to improvement in teacher effectiveness, especially in the most economically and academically disadvantaged schools. The researchers also found that PIL induction was related to increased principal and teacher retention and that PIL induction had the greatest influence on teacher effectiveness when principals participated in the program in their first two years as principals (Steinberg & Yang, 2020).

Finally, a small study using student-level data in an urban district in Wisconsin compared students from schools with NISL-trained leaders to a comparison group of students in the same district over a three-year period. Although there were some differences between the groups—the NISL groups had over twice as many African American students, a third fewer white and Asian students, and lower assessment scores in each year of the study—students in schools with NISL-trained leaders had greater increases in average math and reading achievement over the course of the three years. The differences in gains were statistically significant for middle school students in reading and math and for elementary school students in math, and contributed to reducing achievement gaps (Corcoran, 2017).

Other research examined two programs that included mentoring along with networking and applied learning experiences. The Cahn Fellows Program in New York City offers a 15-month fellowship, including a summer leadership institute, with opportunities for applied learning, regular study groups, and ongoing mentorship. Using longitudinal New York City administrative personnel data and student data, Clark et al. (2009) found that participation in the program was associated with reduced student absences and improved test scores. The effect of program participation on math test scores was estimated to be roughly the same as the effect of a first-year principal acquiring five years of experience.

Another study examined the Greater New Orleans School Leadership Center (SLC), a cohort-based fellows program investing in school-improvement initiatives. The program offers intensive summer institutes, conferences, and workshops; cohort meetings and research services to respond to principals' needs; and learning initiatives through which the principal fellows are guided by SLC staff in working with their schools' staff to develop and implement school improvement plans (Leithwood et al., 2003). Researchers studied 51 participating schools over four years. According to teacher surveys, principals' participation in the program was associated with increases in the quality of their leadership and the conditions in their schools. Further, based on comparisons with similar schools statewide, program participation was associated with gains in multiple measures of student achievement in both English language arts and mathematics—with greater gains in years two and three than in year one.

Design and Implementation Considerations

While the research described thus far points to the efficacy of high-quality principal professional development programs, a few studies with unclear and/or mixed outcomes have raised questions about the effectiveness of the programs studied. However, these programs either lacked critical components of comprehensive programs or experienced implementation challenges. A deeper dive is needed to draw useful inferences about program effectiveness.

Unlike the programs noted in the previous section, the McREL Balanced Leadership Professional Development Program does not include a coaching or individualized support component. The program is designed to enhance principals' effectiveness by teaching school leaders 21 evidence-based leadership responsibilities, such as instructional leadership, developing people, and using data for change. It includes ten two-day, cohort-based professional development sessions delivered over a two-year period. The program expects participants to implement what they have learned in their school sites between sessions and reflect with others when they return for the next session. Two studies found positive outcomes related to principals' self-reported practices and the efficacy and retention of both principals and teachers. However, neither study found effects on student achievement within the two years students were followed (Jacob et al., 2015; Miller et al., 2016). As we have noted, this is a short time frame for tracking student achievement. At the same time, while this program has some of the features of a comprehensive program, it lacks the critical feature of coaching that most other effective programs include.

Further underscoring the importance of high-quality coaching is a study of the University of Washington's Center for Educational Leadership (CEL) program. This two-year program aims to improve instruction by preparing principals to conduct frequent classroom observations, document what they see and hear, and provide useful feedback to teachers. Researchers studied the CEL program in 100 elementary schools across eight districts in five states. They randomly created two groups of schools, one that would participate in CEL and the other that would not, and compared the groups' outcomes during the two program years and the year following. Researchers found that teachers in schools led by CEL participants had increased access to professional development and increased retention rates. However, researchers found positive effects on principal practice and students' English language arts or math scores for only a subset of CEL participants.

Interestingly, the researchers examining the CEL program found that the positive effects that did exist were associated with both principal experience levels and the quality of the coaching that principals received (Herrmann et al., 2019). Specifically, they found that teachers in schools with inexperienced CEL-trained principals rated the instructional feedback and support they received much more negatively than teachers in schools with experienced CEL-trained principals, and while teachers' ratings of experienced principals on instructional feedback and support increased in year two, with positive effects on student achievement, this was not the case for ratings of inexperienced principals. By year two, all of the perceived negative or null effects of the program on instructional interactions and feedback could be attributed to teachers' low ratings of inexperienced principals.

The subset of teachers who did find their principals' feedback frequent and helpful saw positive effects on student achievement, with students experiencing significantly greater gains in math and English language arts scores by year two. The researchers also found that student achievement gains were associated with teachers' and principals' reports of coherence in the school improvement plan. The study found that teachers' reports of principals' competence in providing instructional support, the usefulness of teacher-principal interactions about instruction, and the coherence of school improvement plans were, in turn, strengthened when principals' coaches were more experienced, when their coaching focused more on instructional leadership, and when principals completed more of the coach-assigned activities.

The mixed findings about the CEL program illustrate how the effects of professional development programs can be related to how the programs are designed and how they are implemented. These findings also raise considerations about how to develop quality coaching and what kind of strategies are most useful for supporting principal growth in practices like instructional support and feedback—which may vary for novices and more experienced principals.

Principals' full participation in professional development also matters. While several studies found positive effects for the NISL program, as described earlier, one large-scale study conducted by RAND did not find consistently positive results (Master et al., 2020). While the state with the highest participation rate did have consistently positive results, across the entire sample, only 35% of principals fully participated (ranging from 15% to 49% across states). Although principals were strongly positive about how the program and the coaching helped them to lead their schools better, erratic participation resulted from principal mobility and districts or principals opting out of the study. The researchers also noted that due to accountability pressures, many principals were afraid to be out of their buildings for the required 24 days. This phenomenon was especially notable in the state with the lowest participation rate, where 50% of principals left their positions during the course of the study, thus significantly reducing the already small sample size. As the authors noted, "Low participation rates dilute the measured effects of the intervention in our experimental analysis" (Master et al., 2020, p. ix).

There also were some differences between the implementation of NISL in this study and the Massachusetts and Pennsylvania programs that had consistently positive results, which could explain the different outcomes. Both the Massachusetts and Pennsylvania programs focused on novice principals and were offered to volunteers, and the program was somewhat longer (15–18 months compared to 12 months, with more sessions). Further, since both Massachusetts and Pennsylvania required all new principals to receive mentoring from their districts (see Yirci & Kocabas, 2010), NISL did not need to appoint mentors. In addition, the Massachusetts and Pennsylvania programs trained a Leadership Team composed of key district leaders and principals who were selected to be facilitators. The Leadership Teams received the facilitator handbook and went through NISL as participants, so central office staff were fully exposed to the content of the program and could reinforce it.

A study of the District Professional Development (DPD) program likewise demonstrated how program implementation likely influenced research findings. DPD was designed to improve instruction through a sustained, multi-session, district-based leadership development program focused on problem-based learning. Coursework included collective inquiry and problem-based learning opportunities, but there was no mentoring or coaching component. The program was evaluated in three separate studies using the same quantitative data complemented by qualitative elements. A study comparing principals randomly selected to participate to principals randomly selected not to participate found little average difference in principal knowledge, principal practice, or student achievement outcomes (Spillane et al., 2010). However, qualitative research unearthed many implementation challenges that undermined the research itself.

Neither the DPD program nor the research unfolded as intended. The newly hired superintendent did not support the DPD, and he implemented a separate professional development program for principals. Thus, the principals who did not participate in the DPD also experienced purposeful professional development emphasized by the superintendent and had more support to do so. Further, the DPD was not implemented as planned. Only about half of the 22 principals assigned to participate ever attended, and by the last session, only four principals attended. Further complicating the findings, a few principals who attended DPD were actually assigned to the group that was not supposed to participate. Ultimately, only half of the planned DPD sessions were ever delivered to the dwindling group of attendees. With its implementation challenges and with the group of supposedly non-participating principals also receiving professional development (either through DPD or the district's other program), it is not surprising that no differential effects were found on the practice of principals counted in the participating and non-participating groups. However, for those principals who did attend most of the professional development (a minority of those randomly assigned), a more nuanced follow-up study found positive effects on principal practice (Barnes et al., 2010; Camburn et al., 2016). One lesson is that context matters in the design, implementation, and use of district-sponsored leadership development. Key to the context is district-leader support and advocacy for the learning and a plan for its use within the district's overarching vision and strategy.

A study of the Texas Principal Excellence Program (TxPEP) further illustrates how program design can influence findings. TxPEP was intended to improve student achievement and teacher retention by improving principals' leadership skills. Unlike the more comprehensive programs just described, TxPEP was a set of workshops on business and management practices with no other features associated with high-quality professional development. Researchers compared TxPEP participants to nonparticipating Texas principals with similar characteristics and from similar schools. Using state administrative data, interviews, principal practice logs, and surveys of participating principals and their teachers, researchers found no evidence of program impact on principal practice, teacher performance and satisfaction, or student performance on state tests over the course of the following school year (Hoogstra et al., 2008).

Elements of High-Quality Professional Development

As described above, the research examining well-implemented comprehensive professional development programs has found positive outcomes for principals' learning, practices, and/or influences on school conditions and student learning. Studies that found mixed outcomes demonstrated problems with program design or implementation (e.g., lack of effective coaching or other comprehensive program elements) or experienced challenges with the research methodology (e.g., failure of treatment-group members to participate in the program; small, nonrepresentative samples; lack of appropriate controls or a comparison group). However, in general, positive school and student outcomes were associated with programs that thoughtfully and purposefully incorporated all or most of the best practices in professional development.

Other research focuses on specific programmatic features of professional development. These studies provide more detailed understandings of individual program elements and how they contribute to principals' development. As a whole, these studies strongly suggest that three strategies are particularly important for professional learning: (1) individualized, one-on-one support (mentoring and coaching); (2) communities of principals; and (3) applied learning. Other features of high-quality professional development, such as partnerships between programs and school districts, have received less specific attention in the literature.

Individualized, One-on-One Support (Mentoring and Coaching)

As found in *Preparing School Leaders for a Changing World* (Darling-Hammond et al., 2007) and in the studies reviewed above, guidance and mentorship from expert principals is an important support for principals' learning. Additional research conducted over the past two decades corroborates the importance of mentoring and coaching, while offering new insights into the factors that are most important for mentoring and coaching to support school leaders and help them achieve strong outcomes. These studies have consistently found that mentors and coaches play an important role in building the capacity of school leaders and are the most valued of all professional development opportunities (i.e., Goff et al., 2014; Grissom & Harrington, 2010; Houchens et al., 2012; Lackritz et al., 2019; Wise & Cavazos, 2017).

In two rigorous studies, researchers found that principals who participate in mentoring or coaching programs have higher teacher ratings, greater student-achievement outcomes, and stronger practices (e.g., providing feedback to teachers, discussing actions and goals aligned with feedback) than those who do not participate (Goff et al., 2014; Grissom & Harrington, 2010). In five other studies, principals reported that mentoring and/or coaching helped them to improve their practices in leading instruction, developing people, building positive school cultures and community relationships, managing operations and budgets, and making data-driven decisions (Duncan & Stock, 2010; Sciarappa & Mason, 2014; Tingle et al., 2019; Wise & Cavazos, 2017; Zepeda et al., 2014). Principals in two of these studies attributed improved student outcomes to their mentoring and coaching experiences (Sciarappa & Mason, 2014; Wise & Cavazos, 2017). One novice principal participating in a coaching program explained how it informed her practice:

> I enjoyed the instructional walkthroughs and the conversations I had with my coach regarding the observations. The coach's feedback was very candid and guided my next steps for professional development for my staff and me to enhance student achievement. Each professional development session I delivered . . . supported the teaching practices on campus.
> *(James-Ward, 2013, p. 28)*

Research from the past two decades reveals the mechanisms by which mentoring and coaching build the capacity of school leaders. These mechanisms include socializing novice principals into the profession, providing principals with the opportunity to learn from and collaborate with experts, providing emotional and tactical support to principals, providing opportunities for reflection, supporting the development and maintenance of networks, and building principals' capacities as instructional leaders (Alsbury & Hackmann, 2006; Della Sala et al., 2013; Duncan & Stock, 2010; Gümüş, 2019; Houchens et al., 2012; James-Ward, 2013; James-Ward & Salcedo-Potter, 2011; Lackritz et al., 2019; Lochmiller, 2014, 2018; Parylo et al., 2012; Sciarappa & Mason, 2014; Wise & Cavazos, 2017).

Research has also identified key features that characterize high-quality mentoring and coaching (Alsbury & Hackmann, 2006; Augustine-Shaw & Liang, 2016; Della Sala et al., 2013; Duncan & Stock, 2010; Ermeling et al., 2015; Goff et al., 2014; Gümüş, 2019; Herrmann et al., 2019; Houchens et al., 2012; James-Ward, 2011, 2013; James-Ward & Salcedo-Potter, 2011; Lackritz et al., 2019; Lindle et al., 2017; Lochmiller, 2014, 2018; Sciarappa & Mason, 2014; Silver et al., 2009; Wise & Cavazos, 2017; Wise & Hammack, 2011). These features, which are associated with stronger outcomes, include the following:

- **expert mentors and coaches** who are skilled and well prepared for their roles (e.g., competent in providing feedback and instructional support; knowledgeable about curriculum, schools, and districts; able to develop principal efficacy);
- **coaches with specialized coaching competencies**, including communicating clearly, establishing the relationship with clear expectations and roles, developing trust, and establishing a results-based plan;
- **content focused on developing principals' leadership capacities** (e.g., setting goals, assessing needs, and providing ongoing and tailored support);
- **an appropriate fit between mentors and principals** such that mentors and coaches have the right expertise (e.g., particular skills, school level), disposition (e.g., empathy), and availability (e.g., flexibility, geographic proximity) to best meet the specific needs of the principal;
- **trust between mentors and principals**, with mentors or coaches holding a neutral position;
- **sufficient coaching time**, including an adequate number, length, and duration of coaching sessions to build skills, practice, reflect, and refine capacities in an iterative way;
- **mentor and coach training** provided through coursework, workshops, and internships, and opportunities for mentors and coaches to work with colleagues in professional networks to support each other and share best practices.
- **district leaders' support** for the mentoring and coaching programs and involvement in goal setting for those programs.

Building Communities of Principals

While less extensive than the literature on individualized, one-on-one support for principals, research shows that collegial learning networks (e.g., principal networks, study groups, formal professional learning communities) support principals' learning. They do this by providing opportunities for principals to learn from their peers, build their communication and collaboration skills, and learn new ways of thinking.

Four studies examining PLCs found that, overall, principals participating in structured networking opportunities reported that their experiences helped them to be more responsive to the needs of teachers and staff, students, and their schools (Bengtson et al., 2012; Castro, 2004; DeMoss et al., 2007; Humada-Ludeke, 2013). For example, one study examined the Arkansas Leadership Academy Master Principal Program, a professional development program in which participants advanced through three cumulative phases of professional learning experiences toward "mastery"

(Bengtson et al., 2012). This program relied on peer-learning networks to facilitate reflective practice. Researchers found that having more opportunities for structured reflection and peer learning was associated with higher scores on the participants' portfolios that measured principals' learning.

The research base provides insight into how PLCs can build principals' capacities to lead. Specifically, the studies illustrate that PLCs provide rich opportunities for principals to learn from their colleagues, provide a model of PLCs for principals to re-create in their schools, and reduce principals' isolation. In one study, a principal reflected on how her experience participating in a PLC contributed to her sense of community and her ability to solve problems:

> For me, I think this group has been important because I do not feel isolated. Before, I felt like I was practicing in isolation, because you are at your own school, and you have all these issues that arise, and issues that you do not really talk to your teachers about. So it was nice to have a sounding board, being able to talk and share experiences with people who were facing similar issues. We were eventually able to problem-solve around those issues together.
>
> *(Humada-Ludeke, 2013, p. 96)*

The cohort-based NISL program described earlier further illustrates the power of peer learning and shared reflection in promoting growth. (See Box 3.1.)

BOX 3.1 PRACTICING TO LEAD

The National School Institute for School Leadership is a national, research-based program designed to enhance participants' leadership skills to improve their practice and boost student achievement. Run in close partnership with states and districts, participants are placed in cohorts of 25 to 32 practitioners who meet consistently over 12 to 18 months. During that time, cohorts spend 24 days in a series of in-person workshops with NISL facilitators in which they practice leadership skills and support each other's learning.

Illustrating this approach, during one Saturday morning workshop, the classroom was abuzz as a national facilitator led a cohort through a discussion and role play on coaching teachers. More than 20 school administrators—all active principals or assistant principals in the same urban district—gathered around four clusters of tables, intently reading background information for the next activity: a role play focused on coaching teachers using data from classroom observations. After reading about the context of the role play intently for a few minutes, participants at the tables identified volunteers to play the principal and teacher.

At one table, a first-year assistant principal prepared to play the role of a principal who is concerned to learn that one of her teachers perceives English-learner status as a disadvantage. The principal's observation notes, provided as background materials for the exercise, mention that the teacher focused on managing student behavior at the expense of meaningful content-learning in his classroom. Hesitating, the participant expressed uncertainty about how to begin the conversation. One of her peers assured her that the group is a safe space to "try out" one of the hardest and most important parts of a principal's job and suggested she take a few moments to write down some coaching questions before diving in. Another suggested she try to anchor the role of the teacher to a person she's met in real life to make it easier to engage in the role play.

After taking a few moments, the participant started her "debrief" with the teacher, using the questions she wrote down as a guide to elicit reflections from her role-playing partner. Meanwhile, the other members of the group quietly observed the interaction, taking notes and scanning the guiding questions laid out in their course materials.

After the role play concluded, the table applauded the actors and began to debrief what had occurred. One member of the group noted that she liked one of the questions that the principal had asked and suggested another one that she could have asked as a follow-up. Meanwhile, the facilitator stopped by the table, quietly observing the conversation, and chimed in to ask whether the participants thought having a coach with expertise working with multi-language learners might be helpful. A number of participants nodded, noting that the coach's expertise would be helpful in addressing the concerns with this teacher's practice. The group continued to discuss and debrief before the facilitator called the cohort back together to process their reflections as a large group.

Source: Wechsler, M. E., & Wojcikiewicz, S. K. (2023). *Preparing leaders for deeper learning*. Harvard Education Press.

Notably, research reflects the fact that it can take time for networking opportunities to bear fruit. For example, one study that followed a university-district professional development partnership over multiple years discovered that it took approximately two years before principals saw the benefits of their participation in PLCs: in this case, a greater sense of self-efficacy, increased urgency to improve students' achievement, and a focus on teaching and learning (Humada-Ludeke, 2013).

Applied Learning

Research also consistently shows that authentic, job-embedded experiences tied to principals' day-to-day practice can build principals' leadership capacities. Three studies that directly examined principals' applied learning experience found that these activities—collecting and analyzing student data, facilitating learning opportunities for teachers, conducting classroom observations, and providing feedback to teachers—helped principals build their capacities to use data and enhance communication and collaboration in schools. They also help improve the usefulness of in-school observations, coaching efforts, and teacher evaluations (Carraway & Young, 2015; Cosner et al., 2018; New Leaders for New Schools, 2011). The Arkansas Master Principal Program provides one example of how applied learning through an action-research project supports the development of expert practice. (See Box 3.2.)

BOX 3.2   THE ARKANSAS MASTER PRINCIPAL PROGRAM ACTION-RESEARCH PROJECT

The Arkansas Master Principal Program was established to expand principals' knowledge base and leadership skills in five areas: setting clear and compelling direction, shaping a culture for learning, leading and managing change, transforming teaching and learning, and managing accountability systems. In the last year of this three-year program, the principals conduct an action-research project based on a real problem of practice. These projects are unique to the individual needs of the principal's school and community and are meant to demonstrate the successful implementation of a change in their school. The action-research project culminates in a presentation at the final session of the program in which they share the story of their growth as leaders, their successes, their challenges, and the impact they have had in their schools.

In a light-filled event space in Petit Jean State Park, principals from across the state of Arkansas waited patiently for their turn to tell the story of their work over the past three years of the program. At the front of the room, one principal stood with a PowerPoint presentation as his backdrop. The principal began by telling the room that he started his journey in the program as a relatively new principal. When he accepted his position at a high-poverty, rural school, he saw the need to help teachers develop their capacity to positively impact how students feel at school. He decided to make it his mission to change the culture in the building because, he said, "if you can figure out the culture of adults, that will impact how students feel."

He described his first effort at building relationships with his teachers, something he learned in the program is necessary to shape a culture for learning. He then explained how he and his staff worked together to amend referral polices and think about how student behaviors are often indicative of factors in children's lives outside of school. With limited resources, he pushed his staff to think of alternatives to suspending students, and they created a plan for school nurses and counselors to better support students, all of which led to a more supportive culture for students in the school.

Presenting next was a principal from another district, whose action-research project focused on the goal of making learning more hands-on, so students would be more engaged. In her presentation, she included several photos of her students sitting in rows of desks reading, juxtaposed with pictures of those same students collaboratively building a robot. To make this shift, she described how she and her faculty worked together to re-think curriculum, first doing a brainstorming activity she had learned in the program and bringing in the voices and opinions of her entire staff. Over time, she said, they were able to successfully implement project-based learning, and she described students in her school being "engaged for the first time in a long time."

Another elementary school principal described how she led the development of professional learning communities in her school. She said that teachers now bring student work samples to their meetings where they read and then grade student writing together, a strategy, she noted, that is used in many deeper-learning-oriented schools as an important process for ensuring alignment across classrooms.

In addition to fellow cohort members, superintendents sat eagerly in the audience, waiting to hear more about the good work happening at schools in their districts because of their principals' participation in the program. These presentations are a unique opportunity for leaders to engage with their superintendents, share their success stories, and receive recognition for transforming their schools. After the presentations, each principal met with their superintendent to talk about next steps, plans for the next 30 days, and how the superintendents can be supportive so that the principals could successfully continue the work they started in their action research projects. The morning of presentations ended with a lunch for principals and superintendents, another opportunity to build positive relationships that can help lay the groundwork for continued district buy-in that can lead to systemic change.

Source: Wechsler, M. E., & Wojcikiewicz, S. K. (2023). *Preparing leaders for deeper learning*. Harvard Education Press.

A benefit of applied-learning experiences is that the program instructors can shape the participants' learning process by asking them to examine and consider specific educational elements. In this way, they can build on class discussions related to research and theory, providing a lens for principals to interpret what they are examining in their real practice. One school leader reported about the expanded range of data sources that she and others now use as a result of such a project:

> We looked at student work samples, we looked at the students' grades, [and] we looked at the types of books that the students were being assigned to read in class [and] the types of tasks they were being assigned. . . . So it was a holistic [way of looking at] the multiple forms of data. . . . [I]t was much broader than . . . what we've done in the past.
> *(Cosner et al., 2018, p. 245)*

Another principal in one of the programs featuring applied-learning experiences shared how his participation in the program allowed him to look more deeply at instruction:

> I think I am adept at going into classrooms and seeing the different elements that we have learned. [The program] has made me a better observer in the classroom. Before, I was looking for mechanics, and now, I look for talents, strategies that really make a difference in student achievement.
> *(Carraway & Young, 2015, p. 239)*

Supporting Principals to Meet the Needs of Diverse Learners

Most principal professional development programs examined in these studies focused on critical content such as developing people and organizations, managing change, and leading instruction. A new focus on helping principals learn to meet the needs of diverse learners shows the potential efficacy of providing content addressing equity.

Research shows that principals can benefit from programs specifically focused on meeting the needs of diverse learners. The Ohio Leadership for Inclusion, Implementation, and Instructional Improvement (OLi4) program (described earlier), which seeks to build principals' capacities to be inclusive instructional leaders, provides an intensive and tightly focused approach. This two-year program includes nine in-person sessions per year, individual coaching, and school-based applied-learning experiences. The curriculum and related activities were designed to embody three core values: "promoting equity and social justice; presuming the competence of all learners; and treating access to a high-quality general education curriculum as every student's educational right." It aims to develop six leadership practices: "visioning, using data well, using research and evidence to guide instruction, sharing leadership, coaching teaching, and reflecting on practice" (Howley et al., 2019, p. 5). Researchers studying this program found positive changes in principals' attitudes and practices that were significantly greater than those in the comparison group that did not experience the program (Howley et al., 2019).

IMPACT V, the North Carolina professional development program described earlier, combined coursework with applied learning and coaching. Principals from 11 Title I schools in economically disadvantaged communities participated in the program. They faced complex challenges, including high teacher-turnover rates, inability to hire highly qualified staff or employ instructional technology or curriculum-support personnel, changing demographics, large concentrations of English Language Learners, and—in some cases—physical remoteness in rural counties. The program included a focus on transformational and transformative leadership for equity, with social-justice content in the readings (e.g., texts on culturally responsive practice, tracking, and inequalities in schools and society) and in the assignments—including a sociocultural-analysis project and applications of reflections to the principals' own practices. Coaching was also focused on an equity orientation. Researchers found, in candidates' writings and reflections, that principals' views of social justice and self-reported practices changed due to program participation (Hewitt et al., 2014). In fact, the largest number of transformative leadership codes in the students' capstone analytic and reflective narratives echoed the focus on liberation, democracy, equity, and justice. For example, this participant's views were common:

> I believe that there is a necessity to consider social justice in almost every part of my job description. I must consider these issues in student placement, in grading, in discipline, and even in determining the best bell schedule. I need to ensure that all students have the same opportunity to maximize their potential. I believe that these considerations should be made at the individual level. We should avoid blanket determination of need based on demographics, test scores, or addresses. This is when social justice can go awry. . . . My understanding of the full effect of this principle has been greatly enhanced by the faculty of UNCG.
>
> *(p. 243)*

Similarly, a program sponsored by the University of California, Merced, San Joaquin Valley School Leadership Institute, located in rural California, provided a summer institute, workshops, and networking sessions focused on improving educational equity for students in rural schools with high percentages of socioeconomically disadvantaged students. Principals participating in this program reported that the program helped them develop the skills to change mindsets in their schools and work toward creating environments that value diversity (Castro, 2004).

Researchers have also noted that, given the changing demographics of districts and the kinds of learning opportunities available to principals, more professional development attending to equity concerns and to the needs of specific learners, such as English learners, is needed (Louie et al., 2019; Shields & Cassada, 2016).

Principal Professional Development Research: Limitations and Opportunities

Our conclusions are drawn from a thorough review of the literature that carefully examines study methodologies and results. While some researchers have cited studies finding that principal professional development "doesn't matter" (Coggshall, 2015; Howley et al., 2019), we found that thoughtfully constructed and carefully implemented programs that incorporated the best practices identified in earlier research contributed to principals' knowledge and skills and, when measured with strong methodologies, contributed to positive school and student outcomes.

The studies that did not find consistently positive relationships between professional development and student outcomes either did not include the key features of successful programs (e.g., Texas Principal Excellence Program) or encountered serious implementation problems, including non-attendance of most members of the treatment group (e.g., the District Professional Development Program). A study of one program found that differing degrees of positive influence were related to differences in the coaching quality available to principals. This study also identified differences in principal experience that appeared to affect their skills in giving feedback to teachers (e.g., University of Washington Center for Educational Leadership program). And one program that positively influenced principal perceptions of their learning but not their measured effectiveness lacked a coaching element (McREL Balanced Leadership Professional Development Program).

This recent evidence adds to our understanding of how programs that incorporate the features of high-quality professional development—content focused on instructional leadership, developing people and organizations, and managing change combined with applied practice, mentoring or coaching, and professional communities—influence principals' practice and how changes in practice influence teacher, school, and student outcomes. In addition, the studies offer insights about the features of these elements that appear to matter, such as the kinds of applied-learning opportunities and mentoring supports that are associated with changes in practices and outcomes. Recent research also offers insights about both the need for and the possibilities for constructing powerful professional learning to support equity and social justice, including meeting the needs of diverse learners.

Our review also highlights evidence about design and implementation challenges that can undermine well-intentioned professional development efforts—for example, a failure to adequately select and train mentors, or a body of content that is not appropriate for all of the participants based on their prior experience.

Much of the research on the outcomes of principal professional development programs provides few details on the content and delivery of the professional development provided. Given that most principals have limited opportunities for professional learning, and the opportunities many have had do not incorporate the features of exemplary professional development programs (Rowland, 2017), we need more research that offers more information about program content, delivery, implementation, context, and participants to best understand how high-quality professional development can influence outcomes to add to the knowledge base on effective principal professional development.

The more recent literature also points to questions that have not yet been fully addressed and can guide future research:

- What features and attributes do successful programs embody? How might this vary for different program participants (e.g., novice vs. experienced principals, principals serving in well-resourced vs. poorly resourced schools, principals serving in elementary schools vs. middle schools or high schools, principals serving in large schools vs. smaller schools) and in different contexts (e.g., rural vs. urban districts, large vs. smaller districts, well-resourced vs. poorly resourced districts)?
- What is the dosage (i.e., the amount of time and treatment provided) necessary for professional development programs (including various features of these programs) to be sufficient to support principals? How might this vary by program participants, context, and the combination of learning tools or opportunities?
- How long might it take to see an impact from participation in a professional development program? How might this vary by program participants and context?
- Because the nature of professional development will change over the course of a principal's career, what kinds of professional development would principals most benefit from at different points in their careers (beginners, mid-career, late-career)?
- What are the challenges related to implementation of high-quality professional development programs? How might these challenges be addressed?
- What role can school districts play in facilitating positive outcomes related to principal participation in professional development programs?

- How do principals' experiences over the course of their careers (i.e., the pipeline that leads to the principalship) relate to outcomes of participating in professional development programs? For example, how does having participated in professional development for serving as a mentor teacher or for becoming an assistant principal influence principal practice and related teacher, school, and student outcomes?

Future research can address these questions and others by collecting and analyzing more information when comparing program participants to nonparticipants (e.g., details about program participants and nonparticipants, such as prior preparation, access to supports, experience as a school administrator, and experience as a teacher, and details of the conditions and context program participants and nonparticipants experience) to evaluate program impact.

Answering the questions posed above and paying close attention to the methodologies used, participants, and program implementation would advance the field's knowledge of the best approaches to develop and support school leaders.

4
PRINCIPAL LEARNING AND SCHOOL OUTCOMES

The research we reviewed on principal preparation and professional development shows that both can have a positive influence on principals' knowledge, skills, and behaviors that influence the conditions for teaching and learning. The literature also illuminates some of the important elements of high-quality learning experiences, such as having opportunities for applied learning and clinical experiences. However, most of the research on principal learning analyzes those opportunities in relation to the perceptions of principals and, sometimes, teachers. Few studies have been able to link specific aspects of principal learning—in either preservice preparation programs or in-service professional development offerings—to student and teacher outcomes with appropriate controls for the many other factors that can affect those outcomes. Furthermore, few studies have been able to examine the combination of learning opportunities to which principals have had access, going beyond the efficacy of individual programs.

With the opportunity to link detailed principal survey data to California administrative data for those principals' schools, we conducted an analysis to fill this gap. We linked survey data about preparation and professional development experiences from a representative sample of California elementary and secondary principals to state administrative data files containing longitudinal data on student, teacher, principal, and school characteristics and outcomes, including teacher retention and English language arts and mathematics achievement of students. These data both provide extensive information on each principal's characteristics and experiences and allow us to control for other relevant characteristics of the teachers, students, and schools. (For methodological details see Campoli & Darling-Hammond, 2022.)

DOI: 10.4324/9781003380450-4

Measuring Principal Learning Opportunities

We constructed the principal survey based on the research about both needed knowledge and skills and effective learning strategies that has accumulated over the last two decades (Sutcher et al., 2018). The survey asked principals about their learning experiences and professional development needs for: (1) supporting classrooms focused on deeper learning (e.g., implementing new standards, achieving conceptual understanding of content, problem solving and research skills, and social and emotional development); (2) developing adults as members of an instructional team; (3) redesigning school organizations to better support student and adult learning and community connections; and (4) managing change. The survey addressed both principal preparation and professional development experiences as well as career satisfaction and mobility plans. It was administered by the American Institutes of Research in spring 2017 to a representative sample of California principals, with an ultimate sample of 462 school principals.

Preparation Quality

Using confirmatory factor analysis, we found six factors that represented the 22 survey items associated with preparation: quality internship, applied learning, leading instruction, shaping a positive school climate, developing people, and meeting the needs of diverse learners. (See Table 4.1.) We used the weightings on these factors combined with responses to the relevant survey items to develop scores for each respondent on each of the factors reflecting aspects of the preparation they had experienced. We also developed

TABLE 4.1 Factors and Indicators of Quality Preparation

Indicator name	*Description*
Quality Internship	
Internship Responsibilities	I had responsibilities for leading, facilitating, and making decisions typical of an educational leader.
Leadership Perspective	I was able to develop an educational leader's perspective on school improvement.
Alignment With Coursework	My internship or field experience was tightly aligned with theory and coursework.
Applied Learning	
Problem-Based Learning	The program used problem-based learning approaches, such as action research or inquiry projects.
Field-Based Learning	The program used field-based projects in which I applied ideas from my coursework to my experience in the field.

Indicator name	Description
Collegial Environment	The program emphasized how to create collegial and collaborative work environments.
Leading Instruction	
Instructional Leadership for Higher-Order Skills	The program emphasized instructional leadership (IL) focused on how to develop students' higher-order thinking skills.
Instructional Leadership for Tested Achievement	The program emphasized IL focused on raising schoolwide achievement on standardized tests.
Instructional Leadership for Curriculum	The program emphasized how to select effective curriculum strategies and materials.
Instructional Leadership for Implementing Standards	The program emphasized how to lead instruction that supports implementation of new California state standards.
Shaping a Positive School Climate	
Supporting Diverse Students	The program emphasized how to lead schools that support students from diverse ethnic, racial, linguistic, and cultural backgrounds.
Supporting Social and Emotional Learning	The program emphasized how to lead schools that support students' social and emotional development.
Supporting Whole Child Needs	The program emphasized how to develop systems that meet children's needs and support their development in terms of physical and mental health.
Supporting Restorative Practices	The program emphasized how to create a school environment that develops personally and socially responsible young people and that uses discipline for restorative purposes.
Developing People	
Designing Professional Development	The program emphasized how to design professional learning opportunities for teachers and other staff.
Supporting Learning Cycles	The program emphasized how to help teachers improve through a cycle of observation and feedback.
Recruiting and Retaining Staff	The program emphasized how to recruit and retain teachers and other staff.
Managing Operations	The program emphasized how to manage school operations efficiently.
Investing Resources for Improvement	The program emphasized how to invest resources to support improvements in school performance.
Meeting the Needs of Diverse Learners	
Meeting the Needs of English Learners	The program emphasized how to meet the needs of English learners.
Meeting the Needs of Students With Disabilities	The program emphasized how to meet the needs of students with disabilities.
Equitably Serving All Children	The program emphasized how to equitably serve all children.

Note: Factors denoted in bold.

an index factor across the 22 items. Using the weightings of each variable on this factor and responses to the survey items, each principal received an index score to reflect the quality of preparation received. Scores on both the individual factors and the index were scaled to range from 1 (low-quality) to 10 (high-quality).

Professional Development Access

Our factor analysis of the 18 survey items focused on professional development revealed six factors: professional development frequency and focus on several areas of content: managing change, leading instruction, shaping a positive school climate, developing people, and meeting the needs of diverse learners. (See Table 4.2.) We used the weightings on these factors combined with responses to the relevant survey items to develop factor scores for each respondent to reflect aspects of the professional development they had experienced. We developed an index factor across all of the items. Using the weightings of each variable on this factor and responses to the survey items, each principal received an index score to reflect their access to professional development. Scores on both the subcomponents and the index range from 1 (little access) to 10 (extensive access based on both the frequency and the topics covered by professional development).

TABLE 4.2 Factors and Indicators of the Extent of Professional Development

Indicator name	Description
Professional Development Frequency	
How often have I participated in the following?	
Workshops	Workshops, conferences, or training
Peer Observation and/or Coaching	Peer observation and/or coaching in which I have an opportunity to visit with other principals for sharing practice
Principal Network	A principal network (e.g., a group of principals organized by my district, by an outside agency, or online)
Managing Change	
Using Data for Improvement	The program emphasized how to use student and school data to inform continuous school improvement.
Leading Change for Improved Achievement	The program emphasized how to lead a schoolwide change process to improve student achievement.
Leading Instruction	
Instructional Leadership for Higher-Order Skills	The program emphasized instructional leadership (IL) focused on how to develop students' higher-order thinking skills.

Indicator name	Description
Instructional Leadership for Tested Achievement	The program emphasized IL focused on raising schoolwide achievement on standardized tests.
Instructional Leadership for Curriculum	The program emphasized how to select effective curriculum strategies and materials.
Instructional Leadership for Implementing Standards	The program emphasized how to lead instruction that supports implementation of new state standards.
Shaping a Positive School Climate	
Supporting Diverse Students	The program emphasized how to lead schools that support students from diverse ethnic, racial, linguistic, and cultural backgrounds.
Supporting Social and Emotional Learning	The program emphasized how to lead schools that support students' social and emotional development.
Supporting Whole Child Needs	The program emphasized how to develop systems that meet children's needs and support their development in terms of physical and mental health.
Supporting Restorative Practices	The program emphasized how to create a school environment that develops personally and socially responsible young people and that uses discipline for restorative purposes.
Developing People	
Designing Professional Development	The program emphasized how to design professional learning opportunities for teachers and other staff.
Supporting Learning Cycles	The program emphasized how to help teachers improve through a cycle of observation and feedback.
Recruiting and Retaining Staff	The program emphasized how to recruit and retain teachers and other staff.
Managing Operations	The program emphasized how to manage school operations efficiently.
Investing Resources for Improvement	The program emphasized how to invest resources to support improvements in school performance.
Meeting the Needs of Diverse Learners	
Meeting the Needs of English Learners	The program emphasized how to meet the needs of English learners.
Meeting the Needs of Students With Disabilities	The program emphasized how to meet the needs of students with disabilities.
Equitably Serving All Children	The program emphasized how to equitably serve all children.

Note: Factors denoted in bold.

Analyses

Modeling Teacher Retention

To model teacher retention, we used logistic regression to estimate the odds that a teacher would stay at his or her school for an additional year. We used data about teacher characteristics and their employment decisions for 2016–2017 as the base school year and 2017–2018 as the follow-up school year. We used data about teachers' gender, age, race/ethnicity, years of teaching, educational attainment, and teaching field to control for teacher characteristics that might be associated with their mobility. We also used data about principals' gender, age, race/ethnicity, years of teaching experience, and years of principal experience for those same years.

Modeling Student Learning Gains

To model student achievement gains, we used linear regression to predict student test scores in a particular year. This analysis controlled for students' test scores in the preceding year, along with other student, school, and district characteristics. Student achievement gains were modeled separately for English language arts and mathematics. We used grades three through eight student test data from 2015 as the base year with 2016 as the follow-up year, and 2016 as the base year with 2017 as the follow-up year. We used student scale scores for mathematics and English Language Arts, as well as data about students' gender, age, race/ethnicity, economically disadvantaged status, English-learner status, migrant status, and disability status to control for student characteristics that might be associated with achievement outcomes.

Samples

The samples for each set of analyses differed. For the preparation analyses, we limited the sample to principals who were early in their career (five years of experience or less), assuming that they would rely more on their preparation, in contrast to principals with more experience who might rely more on their experience. This sample for examining preparation outcomes included approximately 200 principals, 6,000 teachers and 59,000 students. The professional development sample included all principals who reported participating in professional development within the preceding two years. This sample included approximately 460 principals, 14,000 teachers, and 314,000 students.

Findings

Principal Learning and Teacher Retention

Principal Preparation

We found that principals' overall preservice preparation quality and all the components of preparation considered in our analysis are positively related to teacher retention. Teacher retention is an important school outcome given the evidence that high rates of teacher turnover harm student learning and create extra costs for districts (Carver-Thomas & Darling-Hammond, 2017). These relationships are statistically significant for overall preparation quality as well as for preparation in developing people and meeting the needs of diverse learners. (See Table 4.3.)

In schools where principals reported that they had received high-quality preparation, teachers' likelihoods of staying in the school were higher (an odds-ratio above 1.0), controlling for other teacher, school, and districts conditions, including district size and spending. To illustrate this relationship, we forecast teacher retention outcomes using our statistical model. If we consider two teachers, one whose principal had low-quality preparation (a preparation index score of 2) and another whose principal had high-quality preparation (a preparation index score of 9),[1] our model projects that a teacher in the school served by the principal with low-quality preparation would have a 78% probability of staying through the following year, while a teacher in the school served by the principal with high-quality preparation would have an 89% probability of staying through the following year, holding all other variables constant (see Figure 4.1).

TABLE 4.3 The Relationship Between Principal's Preparation and Teacher Retention (odds-ratio)

Outcome	Overall Preparation Quality	Quality Internship	Applied Learning	Leading Instruction	Shaping a Positive School Climate	Developing People	Meeting Needs of Diverse Learners
Teacher Retention	1.130*	1.022	1.071	1.068	1.086	**1.148***	**1.111***

$^{*}p < 0.05$; $^{**}p < 0.01$; $^{***}p < 0.001$.

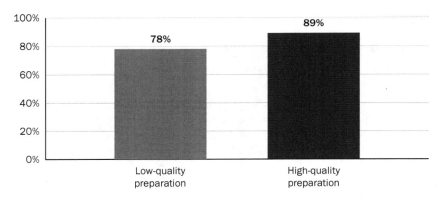

FIGURE 4.1 Predicted Probability of Teacher Retention for Differently Prepared Principals

Two components of preparation were also found to play an important role in teacher retention. We found that principals who reported they had received high-quality preparation in *Developing People* had much higher teacher retention ($p = .017$), as did those who reported high-quality preparation in *Meeting the Needs of Diverse Learners* ($p = .011$). It makes sense that principals who were well-prepared to develop and support their staff would be better able to keep them. That factor includes recruiting and retaining staff, designing professional learning opportunities, helping teachers improve through observation and feedback, managing school operations efficiently, and investing resources to support school improvement. It also makes sense that principals who are better prepared to meet the needs of diverse learners—including English learners and students with disabilities— and to equitably serve all children would be better able to help teachers do the same. Because teachers are more likely to stay when they are able to be successful in meeting the needs of their students, such support can boost retention.

Professional Development

The overall extent of principals' professional development, as well as all the components of professional development, also appear to be positively related to teacher retention. However, none of the relationships reaches a level of statistical significance. (See Table 4.4.)

TABLE 4.4 The Relationship Between Professional Development Factors and Teacher Retention (odds-ratio)

Outcome	Overall Professional Development Index	Professional Development Frequency	Managing Change	Leading Instruction	Shaping a Positive School Climate	Developing People	Meeting Needs of Diverse Learners
Teacher Retention	1.02	1.03	0.99	1.01	1.00	1.02	1.04

Note: ⁻p < 0.10; *p < 0.05; **p < 0.01; ***p < 0.001.

Principal Learning and Student Achievement

Principal Preparation

With respect to student achievement gains, we did not detect a statistically significant relationship between the overall measure of *preparation quality* and student outcomes in either subject area. However, principals' experience of higher-quality internships during their preparation was associated with significantly greater student-learning gains in English language arts (p<.046). Higher-quality internships featured a tight alignment between the field experience and theory or coursework and offered candidates the opportunity to lead, facilitate, and make decisions typical of an educational leader, developing a leader's perspective on school improvement with the support of a mentor. As we have noted, a substantial body of research finds that this kind of internship experience is one of the most important elements of high-quality preparation programs.

To illustrate this relationship, Figure 4.2 shows the differential in the forecasted achievement gains in English language arts of two students at the mean: one whose principal had a low-quality clinical preparation experience (which we define as a Quality Internship score of 2) and another whose principal had high-quality clinical preparation experience (which we define as a Quality Internship score of 9). The difference in their scale-score gains from Year 1 to Year 2 (31 and 35.5, respectively) is equivalent to .08 SD^2 and can be interpreted as an additional month of instruction.[3]

Professional Development

The associations between principal *professional development quality* and student achievement are quite strong and consistent. Table 4.5 shows that the

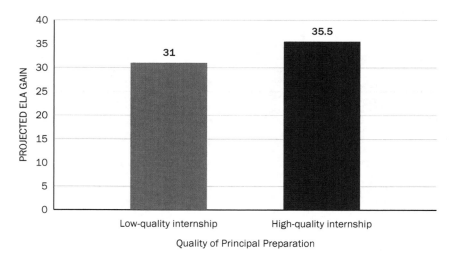

FIGURE 4.2 Projected Student Achievement Gains in English Language Arts (ELA), Based on Principal Internship Quality

TABLE 4.5 Relationship Between Professional Development Factors and Student Achievement Gains

Outcome	Overall Professional Development Index	Professional Development Frequency	Managing Change	Leading Instruction	Shaping a Positive School Climate	Developing People	Meeting Needs of Diverse Learners
ELA	0.817*	0.541	0.476	0.869*	0.615⁻	0.426	0.561⁻
Mathematics	1.281**	0.966**	1.282***	1.176**	0.639⁻	1.129**	0.997**

⁻$p < 0.10$; *$p < 0.05$; **$p < 0.01$; ***$p < 0.001$.

overall professional development access index and each component of professional development are positively related to student gains in both English language arts and mathematics. The overall index is significantly related to gains in both subject areas. Not surprisingly, principals' professional development experiences associated with leading instruction also show a very strong relationship to student gains in both English language arts and math, and the relationship is at least marginally significant in both subjects for "shaping a positive school climate" and "meeting the needs of diverse learners." The strength of the other associations is strongest in mathematics, for which every area of professional development shows at least a marginally significant relationship.

To illustrate the size of the relationship between principals' access to professional development and student achievement, we can consider two students initially scoring at the mean on the achievement tests: one whose principal had little access to professional development (a score of 2 out of 10 on the index) and another whose principal had extensive access (a score of 9 out of 10 on the index). As shown in Figure 4.3, the forecasted difference in gains for these two students, holding student, principal, school, and district characteristics constant at their sample means, is 5.7 scale points in English language arts, equivalent to .10 *SD*, which can be interpreted as an additional month and a half (29 days) of instruction. In mathematics, the 9-point difference in gains is equivalent to .17 *SD*, which can be interpreted as almost three months (55 days) of additional instruction.

Does Professional Development Matter More for Some Principals and Students?

Principal Professional Development and Principal Experience

While the literature suggests that principals may benefit differently from professional development at different points in their careers, studies have not yet addressed how these differences may be reflected in the outcomes of professional development. We examined the relative influence of professional development overall and of each of the components for principals at different stages in their careers: those with three or fewer years of experience

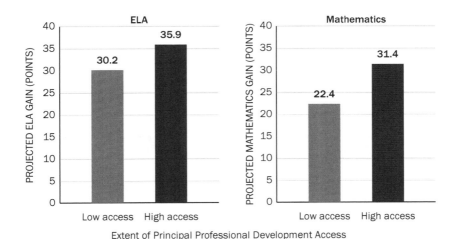

FIGURE 4.3 Projected Gains in English Language Arts (ELA) and Mathematics, Based on Principal Professional Development Access

(early career), those with four to nine years of experience (second stage), and those with ten or more years of experience (experienced).

Early-career principals receive greater benefit from more extensive professional development overall and from a greater frequency of professional development, as well as from specific components of professional development. The greater benefits for inexperienced principals are statistically significant in four areas associated with student achievement gains in mathematics: professional development frequency and professional development for managing change, leading instruction, and developing people. In particular, higher-frequency professional development and professional development in managing change appear to matter far more for early-career principals than for veteran principals who have the benefit of years of experience to rely on.

As Figure 4.4 shows, the student score gains for experienced principals with less extensive professional development are greater than those of novice principals under the same circumstances; however, the gains for students of novice principals with substantial access to professional development are much more dramatic than those of experienced principals. In essence, extensive professional development appears to help novice principals catch up to their more experienced colleagues.

Interestingly, the experienced group of principals (ten-plus years of experience) also appears to benefit slightly more than the second-stage group

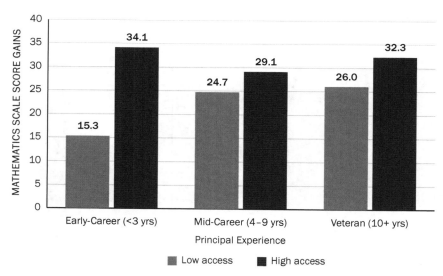

FIGURE 4.4   Student Gains in Mathematics, by Principal Experience, for Principals With Differential Access to Professional Development

(four to nine years of experience). This makes sense when one considers that novice principals have an enormous amount to learn, and those who are much later in their careers, while benefiting from their work experience, are also further from their initial training. Thus, they may lack some critical elements of more recently emphasized knowledge and skills in the areas that professional development provides.

Principal Professional Development and Student Characteristics

Many studies find that school resources of various kinds—dollars, better qualified staff, higher-quality programs—have even stronger effects on the achievement of students furthest from opportunity than on other students (Darling-Hammond, 2019). We wondered whether the effect of principal learning on student outcomes differed depending on students' racial/ethnic backgrounds. This issue is important because the lack of access to high-quality schools, well-prepared teachers, and adequate curricular materials has led to less opportunity to learn and, thereby, lower achievement, for historically underserved students.

We asked the question, "At schools where students are led by principals with access to extensive professional development, is there a smaller gap in achievement gains between historically underserved students of color and other groups?" We defined historically underserved students based on California demographics and achievement trends as Black, Latinx, and Native American students. We compared their gains to those of White students, Asian students (including Filipino students), and other students (biracial students and those who did not report a racial category).

We found that as the principals' experience of professional development in instructional leadership increased, gains in math were significantly more pronounced for historically underserved students of color and, to a somewhat lesser extent, for students identified as "biracial and other" than for White and Asian students.

Figure 4.5 illustrates model predictions for students from different racial/ethnic groups. For historically underserved groups, there was a large, positive difference—estimated to be 11.3 points on the mathematics assessment (just over three months of instruction)—between the predicted gain of students in the school led by a principal with little access to professional development in instructional leadership and peers in a school led by a principal with more substantial access.

Our model also predicts a difference—estimated to be 8.8 points on the mathematics assessment—for students in the Other Race category (multiracial or race not reported). For White students, the predicted gain for those with a principal who has extensive professional development is somewhat

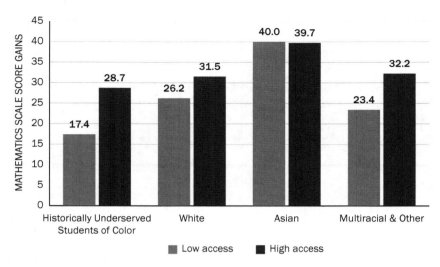

FIGURE 4.5 Student Gains in Mathematics (scale score points), by Race, for Principals With Differential Access to Professional Development in Instructional Leadership

higher (5.3 points) than for those with a principal who has little access to professional development, though not statistically significant.

Based on our analysis, we conclude that access to professional development in instructional leadership for principals could benefit all students, with a greater potential benefit for students from historically underserved groups. Thus, principal professional development may play a key role in reducing racial/ethnic opportunity gaps.

Summary of How Principal Learning Affects School Outcomes

This new analysis—unique in the literature both because of the detail it offers about principals' professional learning and the controls made possible by the extensive multi-level data set—adds to our understanding of both the impact of professional learning and of the importance of quality. Because the analysis is based on a cross-sectional analysis of data at a single point of time, we cannot rule out that other factors may have contributed to the correlations we saw between high-quality professional learning opportunities and teacher retention and student achievement. Nonethless, the evidence is promising.

Our analysis suggests that principal learning matters for both teacher and student outcomes. Teachers in schools served by well-prepared principals are less likely to transfer schools or quit the profession than teachers in schools served by less well-prepared principals. In addition, principals who experience higher-quality internships during their preservice preparation lead schools where students make greater year-to-year gains in English Language Arts, compared to students in schools whose principals did not experience high-quality internships. One way to interpret these findings is that high-quality preparation programs—defined in part by the quality of the clinical internship principals experience—may prepare principals to create a supportive, collegial environment for teachers that encourages them to stay.

Furthermore, greater access to professional development is associated with gains in both English language arts and mathematics, with particularly large gains for students in the schools of novice principals and for historically underserved students of color. In-service professional development programs, especially those focused on instructional leadership, appear to help principals develop specific means to support teaching and learning for those furthest from opportunity.

Finally, our findings suggest that principal professional development can be a key factor in helping early-career principals more quickly reach the effectiveness levels of their more experienced peers. While the relationships we observed do not prove a causal relationship, they are promising evidence that principals' engagement in high-quality preservice and in-service learning opportunities is positively related to the stability of the teaching force and the academic achievement of students.

Notes

1. Principal learning measures were scaled to range from 1 to 10. However, for some of the measures, few principals had scores at the extremes. Therefore, we selected scores of 2 and 9 to represent low- and high-quality learning, respectively.
2. To determine effect size, we converted the difference in gain to standard deviation units by dividing the difference in scale score points by the standard deviation of the difference between Year 1 and Year 2 scores. See Soland, J., & Thum, Y. M. (2019). *Effect sizes for measuring student and school growth in achievement: In search of practical significance*. Brown University. https://doi.org/10.26300/b5as-wr12
3. We calculate the number of days of instruction using the average gain in our sample of students in grades three through eight in California. For each subject, we divided the average Year 1 to Year 2 gain by 180 days of school.

5

ACCESS TO HIGH-QUALITY LEARNING OPPORTUNITIES

As we have shown, high-quality professional learning for principals is associated with their knowledge, skills, and practices and their ability to retain staff and support student learning. But to what extent do principals have access to such learning opportunities?

To understand principals' access to high-quality learning opportunities, we designed and analyzed identical surveys from representative national samples of principals affiliated with the National Association of Secondary School Principals (2019) and the National Association of Elementary School Principals (2020). Data collected from these two groups form a national sample of 836 elementary and secondary principals. We also analyzed two statewide samples of public-school principals surveyed for previous studies that included related questions about professional learning experiences: one from California (2017) and one from North Carolina (2018). The national data offer an overview of professional learning for principals across the country, while the California and North Carolina surveys shed light on how state policy may influence principals' professional learning opportunities. (See Leung-Gagné et al., 2022, for detailed descriptions of the survey methodology and results.)

Principals' Access to Strong Preparation

With respect to preservice preparation, we were able to analyze both national data and data from California. National survey data show that most principals have had at least superficial access to nearly all topics important for building leadership capacity and that access to this content has increased

DOI: 10.4324/9781003380450-5

over the past decade. However, fewer principals have had authentic learning opportunities and well-designed internship experiences. In all these areas, California principals had greater opportunities to learn than principals nationally, likely as a result of recent licensing and accreditation reforms, as discussed in the next chapter, "Principal Development Policy."

Access to Important Content

Nationally, more than two thirds of principals said they have had at least minimal access to all the content areas that research identifies as important for developing principals' leadership capacities. (See Table 5.1.) For more recently prepared principals, the percentage was over 80% in most areas, suggesting that policy changes in the past ten years may have played a role in deepening the content covered in principals' preparation. Changes in access were most pronounced in two areas: meeting the needs of English learners and creating a school environment that uses discipline for restorative purposes ($p < 0.01$).

Nonetheless, learning opportunities were still relatively less available in these areas, with fewer than 70% of principals having had access to learning. Other areas where fewer than 75% of principals had had opportunities to learn include how to recruit and retain teachers, how to support deeper learning, and how to support physical and mental health for students. Principals in California were significantly more likely than those nationally to encounter these kinds of learning experiences, especially in areas associated with preparation to meet the needs of diverse learners. Most striking is that almost all California principals (99%) reported having access to preparation programs that addressed how to support students from diverse ethnic, racial, linguistic, and cultural backgrounds, compared with the national average of 82%. In addition, almost all California principals (97%) had access to preservice training to meet the needs of English learners, compared with just about two thirds of principals nationally (68%).

Access to Authentic Learning Opportunities

While large and growing majorities of principals have access to important content, the teaching strategies they encounter have not evolved nearly as quickly. Few principals have access to authentic, job-based learning opportunities during preparation, and high-quality internships are still relatively rare.

Just over half of principals across the country were trained in a preparation program that was problem based (60%), field based (58%), or cohort based (57%). (See Table 5.2.) In addition, only 17% of principals reported that they had had the opportunity to complete a project at a school other than

TABLE 5.1 Percentage of Principals Reporting Access to Selected Content Areas in their Preparation in California and Nationally

Content Areas	California (n = 461)	National (n = 836)	National Principals Certified in the Past 10 Years (n = 197)	Principals Certified Over 10 Years Ago (n = 559)
Instructional Leadership				
Leading instruction that focuses on developing students' higher-order thinking	93%**	83%	87%*	80%
Leading instruction that focuses on raising schoolwide achievement on standardized tests	93%**	83%	87%	81%
Selecting effective curriculum strategies and materials	91%**	82%	87%*	79%
Leading instruction that supports implementation of new state standards	81%	78%	84%*	74%
Leading and Managing School Improvement				
Using student and school data to inform continuous school improvement	95%**	90%	94%*	88%
Leading a schoolwide change process to improve student achievement	97%**	83%	85%	81%
Engaging in self-improvement and your own continuous learning	98%**	88%	88%	87%
Shaping Teaching and Learning Conditions				
Creating collegial and collaborative work environments	99%**	84%	88%	82%
Working with various school and community stakeholders, including parents, educators, and other partners	99%**	88%	93%*	86%
Leading schools that support students from diverse ethnic, racial, linguistic, and cultural backgrounds	99%**	82%	86%	81%
Leading schools that support students' social-emotional development	95%**	75%	80%	73%
Developing systems that support children's development in terms of physical and mental health	95%**	72%	75%	70%
Creating a school environment that develops personally and socially responsible young people	–	76%	82%*	73%

Creating a school environment that uses discipline for restorative purposes	92%**	67%	77%**	62%
Redesigning the school's organization and structure to support deeper learning for teachers and students	96%**	72%	78%	70%
Developing People				
Designing professional learning opportunities for teachers and other staff	96%**	77%	80%	76%
Helping teachers improve through cycles of observation and feedback	96%**	86%	86%	85%
Recruiting and retaining teachers and other staff	90%**	71%	78%–	68%
Managing school operations efficiently	98%**	91%	92%	91%
Knowing how to invest resources to support improvements in school performance	95%**	76%	81%	74%
Meeting the Needs of All Learners				
Meeting the needs of English learners	97%**	68%	78%**	64%
Meeting the needs of students with disabilities	98%**	91%	91%	91%
Equitably serving all children	98%**	87%	91%	85%

+p < 0.10; *p < 0.05; **p < 0.01.

Note: In the national survey, principals were asked, "During your preparation program, how helpful were professional development opportunities in the following areas at improving your [*topic area*] (if at all)?" Principals could choose from this list of responses: "not at all helpful," "slightly helpful," "somewhat helpful," "extremely helpful," or "N/A I did not have this opportunity." The table shows the percentage of principals who did *not* answer "N/A I did not have this opportunity," indicating that they had at least minimal access to professional learning addressing that topic during their preparation. In the California survey, principals were asked, "To what extent did your leadership preparation program emphasize [*topic area*]?" The table shows the percentage of principals who selected "to a minimal extent," "somewhat," "to a moderate extent," or "to a great extent," and excludes those who responded with "not at all."

Sources: NASSP/NAESP Principal Surveys (2019); California Principal Survey (2017).

TABLE 5.2 Percentage of Principals Reporting Access to Authentic Learning Opportunities in California and Nationally

Learning Opportunities Offered by Program	California (n = 461)	National (n = 836)	National	
			Principals Certified in the Past 10 Years (n = 197)	Principals Certified Over 10 Years Ago (n = 559)
The program used problem-based learning approaches, such as action research or inquiry projects, in which I gathered and analyzed data to help solve a problem.	69%**	60%	64%	57%
The program used field-based projects in which I applied ideas from your coursework to my experience in the field.	76%**	58%	68%⁻	56%
I completed a project in another school requiring that I work with staff to accomplish a goal.	–	17%	18%	17%
In my leadership preparation program, I had a supervised internship or field experience working directly with a principal and engaging in administrative tasks under supervision.	68%*	77%	82%	76%
Among principals who had an internship or field experience[a]				
My internship/field experience adequately prepared me for my first year as a principal.	74%**	46%	53%	44%
I had responsibilities for leading, facilitating, and making decisions typical of an educational leader.	74%**	52%	57%	49%
I was able to develop an educational leader's perspective on fostering the success and well-being of each student and adult in the learning community.	77%**	57%	68%*	53%

Learning Opportunities Offered by Program	California (n = 461)	National (n = 836)	National	
			Principals Certified in the Past 10 Years (n = 197)	Principals Certified Over 10 Years Ago (n = 559)
My internship/field experience was tightly aligned with theory and coursework.	64%**	47%	59%*	44%

$\bar{\ }$p < 0.10; *p < 0.05; **p < 0.01.

Notes. Principals were asked to "indicate the extent to which the following statements about your leadership preparation program are true." They were given options on a 5-point scale, from "not at all true" to "true to a great extent." Percentages indicate the proportion of principals who selected the top two choices: "true to a moderate extent" or "true to a great extent."

[a] In the national survey, only principals who indicated that they had had an internship or field experience were directed to answer the four items listed in this section. In the California survey, all principals were given the option to respond to the four items regardless of whether they indicated they had had an internship or not.

Sources. NASSP/NAESP Principal Surveys (2019); California Principal Survey (2017).

the one at which they were then teaching. This means that most principals learned how to become administrators while serving as teachers, and they did not have the opportunity to undertake an applied learning project in the context of a school at which they were able to take on an administrative role with coaching. And while authentic learning opportunities are becoming more available in preservice training for principals, the gains in access have not been very large (increasing from about 56%-57% to 64%-68% for problem-based and field-based learning, respectively), suggesting that more could be done to enhance the learning experiences of principal candidates.

Once again, principals in California are significantly more likely than principals nationally to have experienced more effective modes of learning during preservice training. These include field-based projects (76% vs. 58% nationally), cohort-based learning opportunities (73% vs. 57% nationally), and problem-based learning approaches (69%, compared with 60% nationally).

While three-quarters of principals (77%) reported having some kind of internship, fewer than half of those who had an internship (46%) felt that the experience adequately prepared them for their first year in the position. Only about half of principals who had internships had taken on responsibilities that are typical of an educational leader, such as leading, facilitating, and making decisions. Access to internships has been increasing over the past decade to 82% of recently certified principals, who were also noticeably more likely to have had experiences that developed their leadership capacities. Nationally, 57% of principals who were certified in the past ten years had responsibilities typical of an educational leader, and 68% were able to develop an educational leader's perspective on improving the school, compared to 49% and 53%, respectively, for principals certified over ten years ago. Even among recently certified principals, though, just over half (53%) felt adequately prepared by their internship experience.

In California, at the time of the survey (2017), somewhat fewer principals had access to an internship or field experience during their preservice programs (68%, compared to 77% nationally), but those who did have an internship reported a more useful experience. Significantly more California principals reported that they were able to gain relevant work experience (74%, compared to 52% nationally) and develop a leader's perspective for supporting students and teachers (77%, compared to 57% nationally). In addition, principals in California were more likely to report that their practical training tightly aligned with their theoretical coursework (64%, compared to 47% nationally). Overall, about three quarters (74%) of California principals thought their internships were a good learning experience for becoming a principal, compared to only 46% nationally. Since the time of the survey, California has launched an induction program for principals as part of a two-tier licensing system, as well as a performance assessment that requires principals to participate in significant fieldwork that engages them in the core tasks of school leaders during their preservice preparation. It is likely that the share of principals experiencing high-quality clinical support may increase as a result of these ongoing policy changes (Reising et al., 2019).

The research we reviewed suggests that internships that provide relevant, hands-on experiences that are integrated into coursework are more effective than internships without these qualities in preparing principal candidates. Yet as our data and other analyses suggest, across the country, internship experiences vary greatly (Hafner et al., 2012). Some candidates have a full-year paid internship in the school of an expert veteran principal, taking on specific leadership tasks in a planful way throughout the year. Others may have an "internship" that is really only a project in the school where they teach or only a few weeks of internship outside of that school (e.g., serving during a school vacation or summer school as an intern) that may not provide opportunities to undertake many of the tasks of a principal.

To further understand the types of learning experiences that contribute to principals' sense of preparedness, we disaggregated the survey findings by those who felt that their internships adequately prepared them for their first year as a principal vs. those who did not feel adequately prepared. As shown in Table 5.3, principals who felt adequately prepared by their internships

TABLE 5.3 Principals' Reports of their Intern Experiences, Nationally

Principals' Reports of Internship Features	Principals Who Had Internships (n = 644)	Principals Who Felt Adequately Prepared by Their Internships (n = 294)	Principals Who Felt Underprepared by Their Internships (n = 343)
My internship/field experience adequately prepared me for my first year as a principal.	46%	–	–
I had responsibilities for leading, facilitating, and making decisions typical of an educational leader.	52%	77%**	31%
I was able to develop an educational leader's perspective on fostering the success and well-being of each student and adult in the learning community.	57%	88%**	30%
My internship/field experience was tightly aligned with theory and coursework.	47%	75%**	24%

¯p < 0.10; *p < 0.05; **p < 0.01.

Note: Of those who had an internship, principals were characterized as adequately prepared if they responded that their internship and/or field experience adequately prepared them for their first year as a principal "to a moderate extent" or "to a great extent." Those who responded "not at all," "to a minimal extent," or "somewhat" were categorized as feeling underprepared. Respondents who indicated that they did have a supervised internship or field experience were asked the extent to which their internships or field experiences reflected the other listed attributes. Principals were given the options "not at all," "to a minimal extent," "somewhat," "to a moderate extent," and "to a great extent." Percentages shown in the table indicate the proportion of principals who responded that their internships included each attribute "to a moderate extent" or "to a great extent."

Source: NASSP/NAESP Principal Surveys (2019).

were much more likely to say their programs provided experiences to a "moderate" or "great" extent that reflected the work of an educational leader (77%, compared to 31% of principals who did not feel prepared); that allowed them to develop a leader's perspective on fostering the success and well-being of members in the school community (88% vs. 30% who felt underprepared); and that tightly aligned the internship or fieldwork with theory and coursework (75% vs. 24% who felt underprepared). These findings suggest that internships that are highly relevant to a principal's responsibilities and are purposefully supported by coursework are perceived by candidates as contributing to their abilities to lead schools.

Variation in Principals' Preparation by School Poverty Level

Our data suggest that access to strong principal preparation programs is not highly equitable. Nationally, principals in low-poverty schools are significantly more likely than those in high- poverty schools to have preparation in creating collaborative work environments, working with various school and community stakeholders, supporting deeper learning, and designing professional opportunities for staff. (See Table 5.4.) Results from the national survey also suggest that principals in low-poverty schools are noticeably more likely than principals in high-poverty schools to have preparation for leading a schoolwide change process to improve student achievement (89% vs. 75%), developing systems that support children's physical and mental health (77% vs. 66%), developing personally and socially responsible young people (77% vs. 66%), creating a restorative school environment (69% vs. 55%), recruiting and retaining staff (71% vs. 61%), and meeting the needs of English learners (68% vs. 56%)—differences large enough to be practically important even though they are not statistically significant.

As we discuss in the next section, policy might make a difference in equalizing access to high-quality preparation. As shown in Table 5.4, nearly all California principals (typically 90% or more) have had access to all the areas of learning covered in the survey, and disparities between principals in low- and high-poverty schools are not apparent. Similarly, California principals' access to programs that offer effective strategies for delivery of preparation is much higher than the national average, especially for those in high-poverty schools.

In comparing geographical differences in access to high-quality principal preparation, we did not find large or consistent differences in access for principals in cities, towns, suburbs, or rural areas or for principals of schools with higher and lower populations of students of color.

Principals' Access to High-Quality Professional Development

Our survey data also allow us to examine the extent to which principals have access to professional development that research has associated with positive school, teacher, and student outcomes. Specifically, we look at principals' access to topics important for building leadership capacity, their authentic learning opportunities, and the degree to which they experience mentorship or coaching.

Access to Important Content

We found that most principals have at least minimal access to professional development that covers important content. As shown in Figure 5.1, 83%

TABLE 5.4 Percentage of Principals Reporting Access to Key Learning Opportunities during Preparation by School Poverty Level, Nationally and in California

Learning Opportunities	National		California	
	Low-Poverty Schools (n = 292)	High-Poverty Schools (n = 84)	Principals Certified in the Past 10 Years (n = 123)	Principals Certified Over 10 Years Ago (n = 105)
Instructional Leadership				
Leading instruction that focuses on developing students' higher-order thinking	81%	83%	94%	95%
Leading instruction that focuses on raising schoolwide achievement on standardized tests	82%	80%	89%	95%
Selecting effective curriculum strategies and materials	80%	80%	91%	91%
Leading instruction that supports implementation of new state standards	79%	74%	79%	85%
Leading and Managing School Improvement				
Using student and school data to inform continuous school improvement	89%	90%	95%	96%
Leading a schoolwide change process to improve student achievement	89%	75%	96%	99%
Engaging in self-improvement and your own continuous learning	93%	87%	97%	99%
Shaping Teaching and Learning Conditions				
Creating collegial and collaborative work environments	87%-	71%	98%	99%
Working with various school and community stakeholders, including parents, educators, and other partners	92%-	80%	99%	100%
Leading schools that support students from diverse ethnic, racial, linguistic, and cultural backgrounds	81%	78%	98%	100%
Leading schools that support students' social-emotional development	77%	72%	92%*	99%

(Continued)

TABLE 5.4 (Continued)

Learning Opportunities	National		California	
	Low-Poverty Schools (n = 292)	High-Poverty Schools (n = 84)	Principals Certified in the Past 10 Years (n = 123)	Principals Certified Over 10 Years Ago (n = 105)
Developing systems that support children's development in terms of physical and mental health	77%	66%	92%*	99%
Creating a school environment that uses discipline for restorative purposes	69%	55%	87%*	95%
Redesigning the school's organization and structure to support deeper learning for teachers and students	80%***	58%	96%	96%
Creating a school environment that develops personally and socially responsible young people	77%	67%	–	–
Developing People				
Designing professional learning opportunities for teachers and other staff	84%~	69%	94%	99%
Helping teachers improve through cycles of observation and feedback	91%	85%	93%	96%
Recruiting and retaining teachers and other staff	71%	61%	91%	91%
Managing school operations efficiently	91%	92%	98%	99%
Knowing how to invest resources to support improvements in school performance	76%	75%	94%	95%
Meeting the Needs of All Learners				
Meeting the needs of English learners	68%	56%	97%	97%
Meeting the needs of students with disabilities	93%	87%	97%	99%
Equitably serving all children	87%	83%	97%	100%
Program Strategies				

The program used problem-based learning approaches, such as action research or inquiry projects, in which I gathered and analyzed data to help solve a problem.	68%	59%	70%	75%
The program used field-based projects in which I applied ideas from your coursework to my experience in the field.	56%	58%	86%	73%
The program organized principal candidates into student cohorts; that is, it defined groups of individuals who began the program together and stayed together throughout their courses.	62%	55%	64%*	77%

*$p < 0.10$; *$p < 0.05$; **$p < 0.01$.

Note: Low-poverty and high-poverty schools are defined as schools in the bottom and top quartile, respectively, of the national school population and of the California school population in terms of the proportion of students eligible for free or reduced-priced lunch. In the national survey, principals were asked, "In different parts of your career (i.e., during your preparation program and on-the-job/in-service), how helpful were professional development opportunities in the following areas at improving your [*topic area*] (if at all)?" Principals could choose from this list: "not at all helpful," "slightly helpful," "somewhat helpful," "extremely helpful," or "N/A I did not have this opportunity." The table shows the percentage of principals who did *not* answer "N/A I did not have this opportunity," indicating that they had at least minimal access to professional learning addressing that topic during their preparation. In the California survey, principals were asked, "To what extent did your leadership preparation program emphasize [*topic area*]?" The table shows the percentage of principals who selected "to a minimal extent," "somewhat," "to a moderate extent," or "to a great extent," and excludes those who responded with "not at all."

Sources: NASSP/NAESP Principal Surveys (2019); California Principal Survey (2017); National Center of Education Statistics, Common Core of Data (2017–18).

National Sample (n = 836)

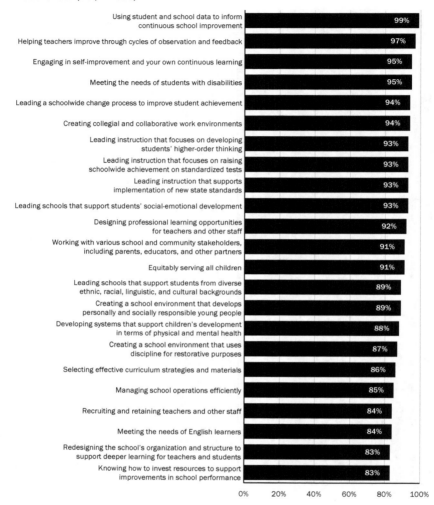

FIGURE 5.1 Percentage of Principals Experiencing Professional Development in Key Topic Areas

Notes: Principals were asked, "While on-the-job/in-service, how helpful were professional development opportunities in the following areas at improving your [topic area] (if at all)?" Principals could choose from this list of responses: "not at all helpful," "slightly helpful," "somewhat helpful," "extremely helpful," or "N/A I did not have this opportunity." The figure shows the percentage of principals who did not answer "N/A I did not have this opportunity," indicating that they had at least minimal access to professional learning addressing that topic in their professional development.

Sources: NASSP/NAESP Principal Surveys (2019).

to 99% of principals reported they had had at least superficial exposure to the 23 topics covered in the survey, most of which were accessed through participation in workshops or conferences.

Access to Authentic Learning Opportunities

Although principals have access to a wide range of content in workshops and conferences, we found that relatively little of their professional development features collaborative and applied forms of learning. As shown in Table 5.5, just a third of principals were able to participate in peer observation or coaching three or more times over the past two years. While more principals (54%) had the opportunity to participate in a principal network at least three times in the past two years, nearly half of principals did not have regular access to a peer network. In California, principals had significantly more access to these forms of collaborative professional development: Nearly two thirds (64%) of California principals participated in a principal network at least three times in the past two years and 43% regularly participated in peer observation or coaching during that time (compared to 33% nationally).

TABLE 5.5 Principals' Reports of Frequency of Participation in Collaborative Forms of Professional Development, Nationally and in California

Professional Development Type	*National (n = 292)*			*California (n = 84)*		
	Never	*1-2 times*	*3+ times*	*Never*	*1-2 times*	*3+ times*
Peer observation/ coaching with an opportunity to visit with other principals for sharing practice	34%	33%	33%*	29%	28%	43%*
Participation in a principal network (e.g., a group of principals organized by your district, by an outside agency, or online)	16%	29%	54%*	14%	22%	64%*

⁻p < 0.10; *p < 0.05; **p < 0.01.

Note: Principals were asked, "Not counting the training you may have received through your leadership preparation program, how often have you participated in the following types of professional development activities during the past two years?"

Sources: NASSP/NAESP Principal Surveys (2019); California Principal Survey (2017).

Despite research showing that mentoring improves principals' leadership capacities, it is not readily available. Nationally, fewer than a quarter of principals (23%) reported having an on-the-job mentor or coach in the past two years, and fewer than half (44%) reported having a principal supervisor (Table 5.6). In addition, underscoring the inequity in access to high-quality learning opportunities, we found that principals serving high-poverty schools were less than half as likely (10% vs. 24%) as principals serving low-poverty schools to have access to an on-the-job mentor or coach. In analyzing responses from the California and North Carolina surveys, we found that while principals from these two states may have more access to an on-the-job mentor compared with the rest of the country, access is still very low (37% in California and 35% in North Carolina).

TABLE 5.6 Principals' Access to Mentors, Coaches, and Principal Supervisors

Principals' Reports of Access to and Support from a Mentor, Coach, or Supervisor	National (n = 836)	California (n = 461)	North Carolina (n = 847)
Percentage of principals who report they were supported in the past two years by a mentor/coach or a supervisor who was provided by the school district.[a]			
Yes, I had a formal on-the-job mentor or coach.	23%	37%	35%
Yes, I had a principal supervisor.	44%	–	–
No, I did not have support via a mentor/coach or a supervisor.	42%	63%	65%
Percentage of principals who had access to a mentor, coach, or supervisor and found it contributed "some" or "a lot" to their success as a leader.[b]			
An on-the-job mentor or coach contributed to my success.	87%*	–	78%
A principal supervisor contributed to my success.	66%	–	–

⁻p < 0.10; *p < 0.05; **p < 0.01.

[a] In the California and North Carolina surveys, respondents were asked, "Have you had a formal on-the-job mentor or coach (other than the mentor or coach in your leadership preparation program) [in the past 2 years]?" and were given the option to respond with yes or no. In the national survey, respondents were asked to indicate if they had an on-the-job mentor, a principal supervisor, or neither. As such, statistical significance between the national, California, and North Carolina results was not tested because of the differences in survey response options.

[b] Principals could select "not at all," "a little," "some," or "a lot" for this survey item. Numbers indicate the percentage of principals who responded with "some" or "a lot."

Sources: NASSP/NAESP Principal Surveys (2019); California Principal Survey (2017); North Carolina Principal Survey (2018).

Principals who had access to such individualized, one-on-one support found it helpful. Of those with access, nearly 87% nationally and 78% in North Carolina said their mentors or coaches contributed to their success as a leader. Two thirds of principals nationally (66%) also said their supervisors contributed to their success as a leader.

Variation in Principals' Professional Development Across States

While we do not have data for all states, it is clear when comparing results of the California and North Carolina surveys that there are major differences in access to significant coverage of important professional development content across states. When asked about content covered to a "moderate" or "great" extent, in all categories but one, California principals reported experiencing deeper opportunities to learn, often by large margins, especially in the categories of instructional leadership, building a positive school environment (which is part of California's school accountability system), and meeting the needs of diverse learners. (See Figure 5.2.) Whereas more than two thirds of California principals had professional learning opportunities for meeting the needs of English learners and for equitably serving all children (67% and 68%, respectively), only 26% of North Carolina principals had opportunities to learn about serving English learners to a moderate or great extent, and only 45% had opportunities to learn about equitably serving all children. Similar disparities were seen with respect to serving children with disabilities (56% in California vs. 39% in North Carolina). Some of these differences may be because California allocated significant funding for professional development while implementing new state standards over several years between 2014 and 2020. At the same time, North Carolina was cutting professional development funding fairly sharply as part of a broader set of budget cuts and policy shifts in the state (WestEd et al., 2019).

In the category of developing people, North Carolina principals reported having slightly more opportunities to learn about recruiting and retaining staff and helping teachers improve through observation and feedback, likely because the state instituted a statewide evaluation system, which did not occur in California. In both states, however, the percentage of principals receiving support for learning about teacher recruitment and retention is quite low (only 38% in North Carolina and 30% in California), a trend also reflected in the national data.

Principals' Reports of Professional Development Needs

Most principals wanted more professional development in all of the topics covered in our survey. As shown in Figure 5.3, the topics in highest demand

California Survey (n=461), North Carolina Survey (n=847)

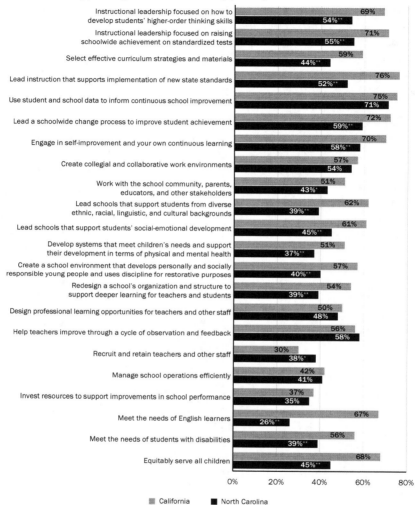

FIGURE 5.2 Principals' Reports of Professional Development Topics That Were Covered to a Moderate or Great Extent

$^{-}p < 0.10$; $^{*}p < 0.05$; $^{**}p < 0.01$

Notes: Principals were asked, "To what extent have the following topics been covered in the professional development related to [topic area] that you have participated in? Topic areas included instructional leadership, leading and managing school improvement, shaping teaching and learning conditions, developing people, and meeting the needs of all learners. They were given the options "not at all," "to a minimal extent," "somewhat," "to a moderate extent," and "to a great extent." Percentages indicate the proportion of principals who selected "to a moderate extent" or "to a great extent."

Sources: California Principal Survey (2017); North Carolina Principal Survey (2018).

National Survey (n = 836)

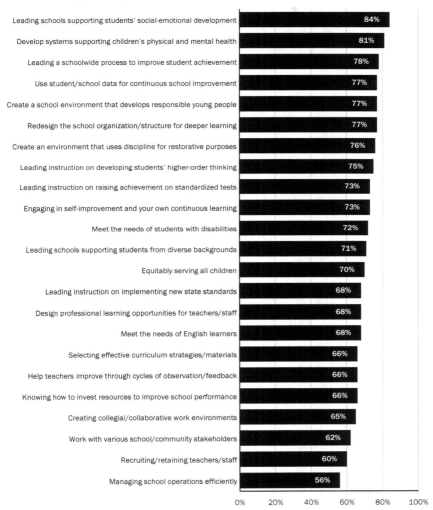

FIGURE 5.3   Professional Development Topics That Principals Want More Of

Notes: Principals were asked, "Would you like additional professional development in this area?" Percentages indicate the proportion of principals who responded with yes.

Source: NASSP/NAESP Principal Surveys (2019).

were related to social and emotional learning and whole child education, including supporting students' social-emotional development (84%) and their physical and mental health (81%), promoting deeper learning (77%), and developing students to become responsible people (77%). More than three quarters of principals were also interested in pursuing professional development to improve student achievement (78%) and using data for continuous school improvement (77%).

Additionally, compared to the national average, California principals wanted more of virtually all professional development topics; over 80% of principals in California wanted more training on each topic. In contrast, fewer than half of North Carolina principals wanted further training in many of the topics covered in our survey. This could be due to their perceptions of the quality of professional development in the state. A recent study of professional learning opportunities in North Carolina surfaced extensive complaints about the low quality of current approaches, often negatively compared by respondents to the much more robust strategies that were widespread before the budget cuts of recent years (Berry et al., 2019).

In comparing principals from schools with different student compositions, we also found that principals of schools with high proportions of students of color (those in the top quartile) were more likely to want professional development in almost all of the topics covered in our survey (Figure 5.4). The topics in highest demand were related to instructional leadership, which includes raising students' achievement on standardized tests (88%), implementing new state standards (88%), and developing students' higher-order thinking skills (87%). Principals of schools with high percentages of students of color were also much more likely than principals of schools with low percentages of students of color to want professional development on equitably serving all children (82% vs. 57%), meeting the needs of English learners (80% vs. 48%), and supporting students from diverse backgrounds (79% vs. 56%).

Despite a high demand from principals for more learning opportunities to build their leadership capacities, 85% of principals reported facing one or more obstacles to pursuing professional development. Nationally, the most common obstacle was a lack of time (66%), followed by a lack of money (45%) and insufficient coverage when they want to leave for professional learning (36%). As shown in Table 5.7, we also found that principals of schools with high percentages of students of color were more likely to lack money for professional development (49% vs. 36% in schools with low percentages of students of color) and knowledge of professional development opportunities (17% vs. 6 %), while principals of schools with low percentages of students of color were more likely to report not having enough time (67% vs. 58%) or coverage to leave for professional learning (43% vs. 25%).

National Survey - Principals in schools with low percentages of students of color (n=294)
and principals in schools with high percentages of students of color (n=104)

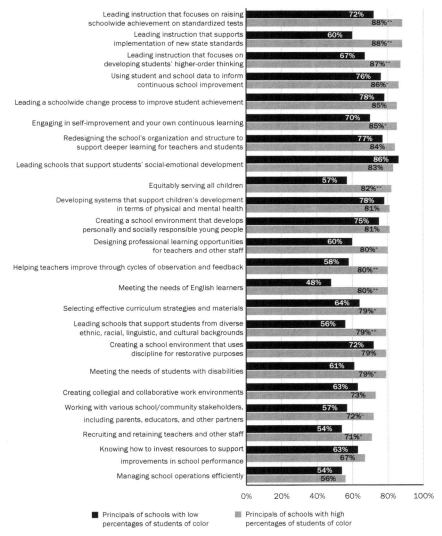

FIGURE 5.4   Professional Development That Principals Want More Of, by School Composition, National Sample

‑p < 0.10; ‑p < 0.05; ‑‑p < 0.01

Notes: Schools with low and high enrollment of students of color are schools in the bottom and top quartiles, respectively, of the national school population in terms of the proportion of non-white students. Principals were asked, "Would you like additional professional development in this area?" Percentages indicate the proportion of principals who responded with yes.

Sources: NASSP/NAESP Principal Surveys (2019); National Center of Education Statistics Common Core of Data (2017–18).

TABLE 5.7 Obstacles Principals Experienced in Pursuing More Professional Development, by Schools With High and Low Percentages of Students of Color, National Sample

Principals' Reports of Obstacles	National (n = 836)	Schools With High Percentages of Students of Color (n = 104)	Schools With Low Percentages of Students of Color (n = 294)
In the school district in which you served during the 2018–19 school year, which (if any) of the following obstacles did you experience in pursuing more professional development for yourself as a school leader?			
I lacked enough time.	66%	58%	67%
I lacked enough money to cover the expense of professional development.	45%	49%	36%
The topics of the current professional development programs were not relevant to my work.	12%	9%	12%
I did not know where to find information about current professional development opportunities.	9%	17%	6%
I did not have sufficient coverage for when I left the building for professional learning.	36%	25%*	43%
I cannot travel outside of the district for professional learning.	7%	4%	8%
I did not experience any obstacles in pursuing professional development.	15%	17%	14%

~p < 0.10; *p < 0.05; **p < 0.01.

Note: Schools with low and high percentages of student of color are schools in the bottom and top quartiles, respectively, of the national school population in terms of the proportion of non-white students.

Sources: NASSP/NAESP Principal Surveys (2019); National Center of Education Statistics Common Core of Data (2017–18).

Summary of Principals' Access to High-Quality Learning

Responses from both national and state surveys show that principals have at least minimal access to professional learning opportunities addressing topics that research has found to be important for building leadership capacity. However, access to effective modes of professional learning, such as authentic, job-based learning opportunities and mentorship, is relatively low. We also found that inequities continue to exist: Principals serving high-poverty schools have less access to some important content in their preparation as well as to key supports, such as mentors.

The survey results also suggest that principals' professional learning experiences vary by state. For example, principals in California have stronger preparation and professional development experiences compared with the national average, and those in North Carolina have much weaker professional development opportunities than California or the national average. These findings suggest that policies matter in determining the quality of principals' learning opportunities. We turn to the policy environment for principal learning in the next chapter.

6
PRINCIPAL DEVELOPMENT POLICY

We know a great deal about the features of principals' learning opportunities that can make a difference in their effectiveness on the job. Survey data show, however, that there is wide variation in the extent to which principals have access to key content on how they can support student and staff learning, as well as the extent to which they experience applied learning with coaching and mentoring that can help them become more skilled. The differences among states and districts in principals' access to key features of preparation and professional development suggest that policy likely plays a role.

In this chapter, we review evidence about policy changes over time and the influence of policy on the learning opportunities principals experience. We answer the following questions:

- How and to what extent has principal preparation and professional development policy changed over the past several decades?
- What are current policy trends, and how do these relate to the features of professional preparation and development that appear to be important for principal effectiveness?
- Can policy influence principal development practices and outcomes? If so, how?

To answer these questions, we reviewed over 170 sources, including government documents, reports by professional associations and think tanks, monographs and books on leadership development and policy, and traditional

DOI: 10.4324/9781003380450-6

journals. We focused on literature since 2000. For studies of policy or program effects, we relied on peer-reviewed sources.

Changes in Principal Development Policy Over Time

Since 2000, a number of studies have identified aggregate trends among state policies that support principal preparation and development. These studies suggest that while noticeable changes have occurred that align state policies with research on principal development, there is still considerable variability in what principals are expected to learn, what they have the opportunity to learn, and what supports are provided for their learning and practice.

State Licensing and Program-Approval Standards

Among the key policy levers controlled by state agencies are the standards used to guide principal licensing and approval or accreditation of principal preparation programs. During the 1990s, new standards for student learning created by subject-matter associations were accompanied by aligned standards first for teachers and then for leaders. Over the past two decades, standards for school principals have become increasingly research-based, have evolved in their content, and have been taken up as tools for leveraging systems of preparation and evaluation (see Table 6.1).

The first set of leadership standards—the Interstate School Leaders Licensure Consortium (ISLLC) standards—were published in 1996 by the Council for Chief State School Officers (CCSSO). In 2008, the National Policy Board for Educational Administration (NPBEA) steering committee revised the standards to create the Educational Leadership Policy Standards: ISLLC 2008. The changes were minimal, primarily making the language more inclusive. In 2015, as technologies, community demographics, and politics changed, the NPBEA assumed leadership over the next iteration of standards, which were renamed the Professional Standards for Educational Leaders (PSEL). The National Association of Elementary School Principals, National Association of Secondary School Principals, and American Association of School Administrators collaborated on the update, which further strengthened the focus on equity.

In 2011, the NPBEA created the Educational Leadership Constituent Council (ELCC) to guide preparation-program design, accreditation, and state approval. These standards included a focus on equity and clinical experience. In 2018, the CCSSO, the University Council for Educational Administration (UCEA), and the NPBEA developed the most recent leadership program standards, the National Educational Leadership Preparation

TABLE 6.1 Overview of Leadership and Preparation Standards

Standard Topic	Leadership Standards			Preparation Program Standards	
	ISLLC (1996)	ISLLC (2008)	PSEL (2015)	ELCC (2011)	NELP (2018)
Mission, vision, and improvement	☑	☑	☑	☑	☑
Ethics and professional norms	☑	☑	☑	☑	☑
Operations and management	☑	☑	☑	☑	☑
Meaningful engagement of families and community	☑	☑	☑	☑	☑
Learning and instruction	☑	☑	☑	☑	☑
Agent of advocacy	☑	☑	☑	☑	☑
Professional capacity for school personnel	☑	☑	☑	☑	☑
Equity, inclusiveness, and cultural responsiveness			☑	☑	☑
Field and clinical internship				☑	☑

Sources: Council of Chief State School Officers. (2008). Educational Leadership Policy Standards: 2008; National Policy Board for Educational Administration (NPBEA). (2011). Educational Leadership Program Recognition Standards: 2011 ELCC Building Level; National Policy Board for Educational Administration. (2015). Professional Standards for Educational Leaders 2015; National Policy Board for Educational Administration. (2018). National Educational Leadership Preparation (NELP) Program Recognition Standards: Building Level.

(NELP) Program Recognition Standards, which reinforced a focus on equity and added a major emphasis on clinical practice.

Trends Over Time

State principal-licensure rules have evolved considerably over time. An analysis comparing 2002 and 2004 (Adams & Copland, 2005) characterized the standards as "unbalanced across states and misaligned with today's ambitions for school leaders" (p. 2). At that time, only six states emphasized knowledge and skills focused on student learning. While 28 more states included some mention of student learning, half of the states did not specify the intended knowledge or skills, and "totally missing" from requirements were such elements as "use of learning assessments, indicators and feedback mechanisms indicating progress toward goals, promoting peer evaluation of teaching, or fostering knowledge of learning goals among teachers" (p. 29).

By 2014, 35 states had revised their licensure standards, and all 50 states plus Washington, DC, had adopted or adapted the ISLLC standards, focusing more clearly on supports for student learning (Vogel et al., 2014). In addition to adoption of the standards, most states required:

- a valid educator license (40 states);
- experience in an educational setting (32 states, but only eight required a teaching license);
- completion of a preparation program (50 states, with 34 states requiring a master's degree); and
- passage of an assessment (30 states, with 19 states following an initial license exam with an advanced exam).

As state licensure requirements evolved, the rates at which principals completed preservice preparation programs increased. Between 1990 and 2000, there was a sharp increase in the proportion of principals reporting they had participated in a preparation program before becoming a principal, with a slower increase between 2000 and 2012 after a brief dip near the beginning of the decade. By 2012, between 50% and 60% of urban, suburban, and rural principals had experienced preparation before becoming a principal (Manna, 2015). Updated data from the National Teacher and Principal Surveys show that by 2015-2016, 64% of urban principals and 60% of suburban principals experienced preparation before entering the principalship, as compared to only 52% of rural principals. While these data suggest progress, they also indicate there is a long way to go before the United States has a fully prepared principal force.

High-leverage Policies

In 2015, the University Council for Education Administration (UCEA) used the research on strong principal preparation and development to develop criteria for examining state licensing and program-approval policies (Anderson & Reynolds, 2015). The researchers distinguished between high-leverage policies (those strongly grounded in the research on principal effects) and regulatory policies (those that are required but less influential for supporting strong principal performance). (See Table 6.2.) High-leverage program-approval policy criteria include proactive candidate recruitment and selection, clinically rich internships, strong partnerships between institutions of higher education and districts, and regular state oversight with feedback. In drawing on the research to define these criteria, they noted, for example, that effective clinical experiences are deliberately structured, are tightly integrated with curriculum, are supervised by an expert veteran, and offer engagement in core leadership responsibilities over at least 300 hours of clinical work. High-leverage candidate-licensure-policy criteria include experience and education requirements.

TABLE 6.2 UCEA Criteria for Evaluating State Principal Preparation Policies

Program-Approval Criteria	No. of States (Including DC)
1. Has an Explicit Selection Process: High Leverage	6
1.1. Includes a plan for targeted recruitment into program	1
1.2. Utilizes performance-based assessments for principal candidates	6
2. Program Standards: Regulatory	51
2.1. Has adopted or adapted school leadership standards from a nationally recognized organization	51
3. Clinically Rich Internship: High Leverage	20
3.1. Is deliberately structured	21
3.2. Tightly integrates fieldwork with curriculum	16
3.3. Engages candidates in core leadership responsibilities	18
3.4. Provides supervision by an expert mentor	25
3.5. Enables exposure to multiple sites and/or diverse populations	18
3.6. Requires 300+ hours of field-based experience	14
4. University–District Partnerships: High Leverage	16
4.1. Provides a clinically rich internship experience	13
4.2. Enables district-provider collaboration on selection	10
4.3. Aligns district needs and program design	16
5. Program Oversight: High Leverage	38
5.1. Requires state review at specified intervals	26
5.2. Includes documentation and/or site visit in plan for initial program oversight	32
5.3. Requires oversight team to have relevant experience and training	30
5.4. Includes feedback mechanism to improve practice	30

Candidate Licensure Criteria	
1. Experience Requirements: High Leverage	50
1.1. Requires 3+ years of teaching experience	39
1.2. Requires a master's degree in educational leadership or a related field	20
1.3. Requires completion of an accredited and/or approved preparation program	43
2. Assessment Requirements: Regulatory	36
2.1. Requires completion of assessments based on national or state standards	34
2.2. Includes a portfolio review of practice in assessment	6
3. Licensure Renewal: Regulatory	47
3.1. Requires renewal with a distinction between license types	34
3.2. Requires continuing education activities	45

Source: Anderson and Reynolds (2015).

Applying these criteria to the 50 states, the study came to sobering conclusions: While all states had adopted nationally recommended program standards and nearly all required some experience and training to become a principal, as of 2015 fewer than half of the states required a rigorous selection process, a clinically rich internship, district-university partnerships, an advanced degree in educational leadership, or a performance-based assessment for licensure. Only two states—Illinois and Tennessee—met all five of the high-leverage criteria, while 11 states met none of the high-leverage criteria.

The authors noted that states are more likely to legislate requirements for principal licensure than for principal preparation program approval, despite the fact that more of the features required for approval of principal preparation programs have strong support in the research base. Similarly, regulatory policies are more likely to be legislated than high-leverage policies that require greater change in practice in the field, often with financial implications for programs and/or candidates. One of the states that adopted a set of high-leverage policies for principal preparation is North Carolina (see Box 6.1.)

BOX 6.1   NORTH CAROLINA'S PRINCIPAL FELLOWS PROGRAM

In 1993, North Carolina launched one of the nation's most ambitious programs to improve school leadership training: the state's Principal Fellows Program. The program provides competitive, merit-based scholarship loans to individuals seeking a master's degree in School Administration and a principal position in North Carolina public schools. In their first year, fellows receive $30,000 to assist them with tuition, books, and living expenses while they study full time. In their second year, fellows receive an amount equal to the salary of a first-year assistant principal, as well as an educational stipend, and undertake a full-time school-based internship during which they work under the supervision and mentorship of a veteran principal. Fellows' yearlong internships can provide meaningful and authentic learning opportunities that research indicates are critical in principal development (Sutcher et al., 2017). Fellows are required to maintain employment as a principal or assistant principal in North Carolina for four years to repay their scholarship loans.

While the North Carolina survey we described in the previous chapter did not include questions about preservice training, other outcome data suggest positive effects of the program. As of 2015, 1,300 principal fellows had completed the program; nearly 90% of fellows graduated and completed their four-year service commitments (Bastian & Fuller, 2016). Research on the effectiveness of graduates who go on to serve in schools found that fellows have more positive impacts on student absences, teacher retention, and school working conditions than other North Carolina principals (Bastian & Fuller, 2016; University of North Carolina Academic and University Programs Division, 2015). Furthermore, more than two thirds of principal fellows assume administrative positions immediately after their training, about twice as many as graduates from other programs, and within three years of completing their training, nearly 80% have become administrators, about twice as many as in other pathways. By three years after graduation, only 14% of principal fellows have left teaching or administration in the state, about half the rate of graduates of other programs (Darling-Hammond et al., 2019).

In June 2020, the Principal Fellows Program, which funds principals directly, was merged with the Transforming Principal Preparation Program (TP3), a competitive annual state grant of about $4 million that supported six North Carolina institutions of higher education. Programs applying for a TP3 grant must demonstrate how the program implements research-based practices to support effective preparation of principals for high-need schools. In practice, principal preparation programs selected for the Principal Fellows Program grant include the following ten features: (1) targeted efforts to recruit participants; (2) rigorous selection of participants; (3) implementation of a cohort model; (4) incorporation of professional leadership standards woven through all aspects of the program; (5) varied and frequent feedback from colleagues, faculty, mentors, and coaches; (6) an emphasis on inquiry-based, hands-on, and authentic learning experiences; (7) project-based learning methods and fieldwork to prepare participants to work in high-need communities and schools; (8) a full-time internship that allows participants to experience administrative responsibilities under the supervision of a mentor principal; (9) collaborative partnerships with districts; and (10) continuous review and program improvement activities. Aspiring principals who are accepted into the program receive a forgivable loan, a ten-month paid internship, and assistance for books (Gates et al., 2020).

Manna (2015) examined policies leveraging stronger quality and noted progress in several policy areas, including the following:

- Using **standards to create greater coherence** among the many policies and initiatives that influence preparation and practice. For example,

Delaware used the ISLLC standards to guide policy and principal experiences "from pre-service to induction to career" (Augustine et al., 2009, p. 76), including professional development and principal evaluation. Iowa used the standards as the foundation for principal licensing, evaluation, mentoring, and other training. Kentucky used the standards as "the guiding doctrine" for preparing new principals, inducting them into their schools and evaluating their work.

- Encouraging **proactive recruitment** of potential principals rather than just selecting from among those who have entered credentialing programs. In Florida, for example, whereas anyone can apply to enter a university program to acquire an assistant principal credential (Level 1 certification), the state has made school districts responsible for identifying and developing candidates for the principal role (Level 2 certification). North Carolina's Principal Fellows Program supports internships for prospective principals who are proactively selected by districts that partner with university-based master's programs to provide placements with mentoring integrated into the coursework.

- Engaging in **more assertive program approval** of principal preparation programs to leverage improvement, including designing a serious process of program approval and sunsetting old programs when new, higher standards are introduced, allowing only those that meet the standards to admit students. For example, Illinois and Kentucky required their preparation programs to adopt new standards, research-based content, and well-designed internships to continue operations.

- Making **licensure more performance-based.** Principal performance assessments, first launched in Connecticut in the 1990s, represent a powerful new trend in state licensure. Massachusetts became the second state to move beyond paper-and-pencil tests with its new Performance Assessment for Leaders (MA-PAL), which reflects the authentic work of school leaders, aligned with state indicators (see, for example, Orr & Hollingworth, 2020). By 2015, California, Delaware, and Ohio required candidates for advanced licensure to assemble portfolios of artifacts based on their practice. Since then, California has launched a state-run Administrator Performance Assessment for preservice principals (Reising et al., 2019). These assessments have triggered principal preparation programs to revamp their curricula and teaching methods to engage principals in research-based clinical learning about how to support teacher development and school improvement (Orr & Hollingworth, 2018).

- Leveraging **more systemic professional development** to meet state and local policy and practice shifts, such as those associated with new student standards, as Kentucky did. States with leadership academies—such as Delaware, Kentucky, Massachusetts, Minnesota, New Mexico, and North

Carolina—have a vehicle for such focused training around pressing needs. Six states developed systemic statewide initiatives with the National Institute for School Leadership (NISL), which offers a program based on the ISLLC standards and research on leadership across various fields. As we described in the chapter "Principal Professional Development," for example, Pennsylvania partnered with NISL to develop a statewide program for novice principals and assistant principals that, since 2005, has helped improve the skills and effectiveness of hundreds of principals across the state (see Box 6.2).

Finally, as we discovered in our literature synthesis, mentoring and coaching are critical elements of effective professional development that have been increasing over time. Between 2000 and 2012, the proportion of principals

---

BOX 6.2   PENNSYLVANIA'S FOCUSED APPROACH TO INDUCTION POLICY

A key area of state principal development policy is principal induction. As of 2016, 20 states had introduced principal induction requirements (Goldrick, 2016), generally mandating that new principals complete these requirements within two years of their initial employment. Seventeen states require mentoring for new principals, and 15 require coursework. Of these, three states—Hawaii, Pennsylvania, and South Carolina—require specific coursework.

All school principals are required to participate in the Pennsylvania Inspired Leadership (PIL) program within their first five years of employment. The program requires principals to take formal coursework tied to an action-research project focused on the state's leadership standards through the NISL. The coursework provides principals with training to examine school data to identify school, teacher, and individual student needs and with the strategic planning tools to implement a vision of high-quality teaching and learning (Steinberg & Yang, 2020).

A study of this program over an eight-year period from 2008–2009 to 2015–2016 found that principals' participation—especially during their first two years as a principal—was associated with improved student achievement and teacher effectiveness in mathematics, with the strongest relationships concentrated among the most economically and academically disadvantaged schools in Pennsylvania. In addition, teacher turnover declined by approximately 18% in the years following principals' participation in the program (Steinberg & Yang, 2020).

reporting they received such supports increased from 50% to over 60% for urban principals, from 40% to just over 50% for suburban principals, and from about 35% to nearly 50% for rural or small-town principals (Manna, 2015). Updated data analyses we conducted show that these numbers remained stable in 2017–2018. As with preservice preparation, these indicators suggest there is still a long way to go to ensure such supports for all principals.

Trends Reflected in State Plans Under the Every Student Succeeds Act

Another glimpse of trends can be seen in states' plans for leadership development in response to the federal Every Student Succeeds Act (ESSA), enacted in December 2015 and implemented in the following year. When ESSA was enacted, all states indicated that they would invest in school leadership under one or more provisions of the law. These provisions include Title I funding for high-poverty schools generally, as well as targeted funds for schools identified for intervention and improvement; Title II funding for professional development, offering states an optional 3% state set-aside for leadership development initiatives; and funding from other titles in the law for leadership development focused on particular kinds of programs.

All 50 states, plus Washington, DC, and Puerto Rico, planned to invest in leadership development, and more than 40 acknowledged the importance of leadership in their plans to improve struggling schools and create a pipeline of diverse principals and more equitable distributions of educators (New Leaders, 2018). (See Figure 6.1.) These equity-oriented plans are noteworthy because there has been little historic statewide focus on the need for leadership in schools serving the neediest students. More than 40 states proposed to invest in leadership for high-poverty schools, for those targeted for improvement under the law, and for those engaged in turnaround efforts. Some, like Vermont, planned to invest in training for principals to advance equitable access to great teachers. Many also focused on the diversity of the leadership workforce. For example, Montana planned to support Montana State University's Indian Leadership Education Development Project to recruit American Indian educators into leadership positions for schools serving large populations of Indigenous students.

About half of the states planned to use the Title II set-aside for school leadership; more than 20 planned to invest these funds in improved preservice preparation and/or in improved induction for new principals. Smaller numbers (fewer than 12) were planning to invest in principal pipelines by focusing on assistant principals, strengthening school leadership teams, or improving principal supervisor roles or management systems. In Texas, for example, districts can compete for additional Title I dollars to support their

1. Prioritizing Excellent Instructional Leadership

- 50 states, including Washington, DC, and Puerto Rico, intend to invest in leadership.
- 24 states plan to use the Title II 3% set-aside for school leadership.
- 46 states identify, require, or prioritize evidence-based strategies to support school leadership or school improvement.

2. Advancing Diverse, Equity-Focused Leadership

- Eight states plan to upgrade school leadership standards, including to align with or adapt the Professional Standards for Education Leaders.
- 41 states acknowledge leadership in their plans to improve the lowest-performing schools; those with large, persistent achievement gaps; or other high-need schools.
- 41 states address leadership in educator equity plans.

3. Distributing Leadership and Building a Leadership Pipeline

- 36 states are investing in teacher leadership.
- Ten states are focused on strategically rethinking and investing in assistant principals.
- Nine states are advancing shared leadership models by strengthening school leadership teams.

4. Strengthening and Innovating Preservice Principal Preparation

- 14 states are investing in promising new principal residencies and academies, including innovative models operated by the state, districts, or nonprofits.
- 21 states are expanding high-quality existing preparation programs.
- 13 states are upgrading principal certification or licensure.

5. Focusing on and Reimagining On-the-Job Principal Support

- 21 states are investing in induction support for new school leaders.
- 16 states will strengthen performance management systems for principals, including by tying evaluation results to tailored, high-quality professional development and support.
- 11 states are rethinking and investing in principal supervisor roles and management systems.

FIGURE 6.1 Analysis of Trends in State Policy Plans Under ESSA

Source: New Leaders (2018)

high-need schools, including by building the instructional leadership capacity of school leadership teams.

Another analysis of ESSA plans (De Voto & Reedy, 2019) noted that some states proposed efforts to disseminate knowledge about equity-oriented leadership strategies among practitioners and preparation providers. For example, Nebraska has organized an Educational Leadership Learning Council to advance equity-focused conversations and activities across the state, identify levers associated with ensuring equitable opportunity and access, and support school leaders. New York's plans focused on attracting more diverse, culturally competent, and highly effective leaders; providing opportunities for aspiring leaders to improve their practice over time; and creating communities of practice to share effective leadership skills among peers.

Can Policy Influence Practice?

While common directions can be seen in state leadership-development policy, considerable variability still exists in what occurs across states.

Competing Guidance and its Influence On Policy and Perceived Quality

Part of the reason for variability may be the differences in policy recommendations that have emanated from organizations with ideologically distinct perspectives. Recommendations from researchers and professional organizations, such as University Council for Education Administration), have emphasized the use of standards, the development of principal pipelines, and the creation of policies to leverage stronger preparation. Meanwhile, recommendations from conservative think tanks have emphasized market-based perspectives focused on selecting individuals without prior education experience, bypassing or reducing certification requirements, and focusing instead on evaluations that would dismiss those who fail to produce results (e.g., Finn et al., 2003; Levine, 2005; for responses, see Young et al., 2005).

These differences in perspective show up in state policies. All 50 states are engaged in policymaking to improve principal quality, while most are pursuing bimodal approaches—both stronger requirements for programs and licensing based on new standards, and alternative pathways that admit individuals who do not encounter these programs or standards on their entry into the profession. Even as a growing number of states are pursuing new leadership standards, licensure requirements, clinical approaches, coaching and mentoring, team training, and academies, the fastest-growing sector is online, often for-profit, training of much lower quality.

Evidence suggests that distinctive policies lead to noticeably different principal learning conditions across states and produce different perceptions of training quality. For example, as Colorado policies have allowed growing flexibility in whether and how principals are trained prior to entry, a recent survey of school superintendents about principal training models found that "over half (51%) of Colorado superintendents selected individual enrollment in an exclusively online program as the least effective delivery model," followed by state-approved alternative certification programs. When asked about the ideal model, 39% of Colorado superintendents selected university-operated cohort-based programs offered in their districts, followed by university-district partnership cohort courses leading to a credential (22%) (Weiler & Cray, 2012, p. 69). In contrast to the wide variability and dissatisfaction in Colorado, an implementation study of the new, more rigorous, and uniform state principal preparation endorsement law in Illinois (Box 6.3) reported high marks from superintendents about the quality of principal preparation (White et al., 2016).

BOX 6.3 ILLINOIS' COMPREHENSIVE APPROACH TO TRANSFORMING PREPARATION

Comprehensive changes in Illinois produced substantial changes in principal preparation program designs, curriculum, and clinical experiences (Hunt et al., 2019; White et al., 2016; Young & Reedy, 2019). Between 2000 and 2015, the state terminated programs leading to a General Administrative Certificate and established a targeted pre-k-12 principal endorsement designed specifically to prepare principals to address the leadership challenges of today's schools. It also requires:

- formal partnerships between principal preparation programs and districts, with both engaging in program design, delivery, and continuous improvement;
- rigorous selection processes that include interviews and portfolios showing previous leadership experiences, interpersonal skills, and impact on student growth;
- alignment with local and national standards for leading pre-k-12, including student subgroups (special education, English learners, gifted, and early childhood);
- a yearlong, performance-based internship designed to provide candidates with authentic leadership experiences in areas shown to improve student learning;
- competency-based assessments of candidate performance aligned with ISLLC standards and Southern Regional Education Board critical success factors;
- collaborative supervision, support, and assessment of candidates by faculty supervisors and mentor principals who meet established qualifications and training requirements;
- an exam administered to all candidates by the state prior to being awarded the pre-k-12 principal endorsement.

The results of these changes for program designs were substantial. Just a year after the final sunsetting of all existing principal preparation programs in Illinois, the Consortium for Chicago School Research and the Illinois Education Research Council conducted an implementation study of the state's new principal preparation law, documenting changes in:

- **Recruitment and enrollment:** Enrollments in preparation programs dropped as programs moved from general administrative training to a principal-specific focus. Many fully online programs chose to discontinue. Stakeholders generally viewed this as a shift from quantity to quality that benefited principal preparation.
- **Partnerships:** The redesign strengthened partnerships between programs and districts.
- **Curriculum:** Programs revamped curricula and internships toward greater focus on instructional leadership, while attention to organizational management continued.
- **Attention to diversity:** Special-education, early-childhood, and English-learner student populations received increased coverage in both coursework and internships.
- **Mentoring and internships:** The new internship requirements—including instructional leadership opportunities, direct leadership, and experiences working with many types of students—were generally viewed as deeper, clearer, and more authentic.
- **Continuous improvement:** An increased focus on continuous improvement highlighted the importance of better data collection and analysis of candidate outcomes (White et al., 2016).

The Illinois story represents a sustained focus over two decades on principal preparation and development as a lever to improve student learning outcomes at scale statewide, and it provides a number of implementation lessons (Young & Reedy, 2019). These include:

Stakeholder involvement in the legislative process. By passing an initial joint resolution in the state legislature, principal preparation advocates established the authority, in a state legislative task force, to make recommendations to the legislature. The joint resolution included as members of the task force the State Board of Education and the Board of Higher Education; school principals; education leadership faculty; private and public college and university education deans; teachers; superintendents; school board members; professional teacher and principal

organizations; and representatives of student populations, such as special education and preschool, from across the state.

Time and process for genuine collaboration. Although the task force
finished its recommendations to the state legislature in under a year, it
spent an additional year in design teams and public hearings to work out
the recommendations in detail.

Evidence base. The task force reviewed a wealth of available research and
data on principal preparation programs and generated new data through
surveys and other research, which helped with the program redesign policy efforts and to communicate with external audiences.

Resources. As the task force's work progressed and became visible, it was
able to attract funding from the state and philanthropic organizations to
support innovation and dissemination.

Implementation Affects Outcomes

Studies have begun to note the ways in which state design and implementation
of policies matter. In 2013, the *Journal of Research in Leadership Education*
published a special issue focused on university programs' responses to state
policy mandates in Alabama, Florida, Georgia, New Jersey, and North Carolina. Each of the states required all university preparation programs to review
and redesign their programs. All of the processes emphasized developing university-district partnerships and increasing the amount and intensity of field
experiences, and all but Florida's were cooperatively launched. An analysis of
the cases noted three factors that were linked to the quality of implementation:

1. The degree of comprehensiveness: More comprehensive reforms that
jointly and coherently influenced the many elements of program quality
were more successful.
2. The degree of organization in the rollout process: When state agencies
were better organized, implementation was stronger and the desired
changes more readily achieved.
3. The nature of communication and collaboration: Collaborative approaches
with regular, two-way communication between programs and state agencies were more effective (Phillips, 2013).

While the reforms had noticeable impact, Young (2013) voiced concern
about state agencies as drivers of change, as state agency resources were
sharply declining due to the Great Recession of 2008: "As state departments
of education shrink and their levels of expertise are reduced, it is questionable

whether they have the capacity to support, monitor, and evaluate meaningful and sustainable program change" (p. 252). However, state funding grew in the subsequent years of recovery, and evidence has grown about the possibilities for policy-induced improvements as states have increasingly infused research-based professional standards into their systems. Three years later, Young et al. (2016) described how states were using standards "to set expectations, guide improvements, and influence practice" (p. 38). The well-documented research base for what are now the National Educational Leadership Program (NELP) standards and the Professional Standards for Educational Leaders (PSEL) has been a means to infuse knowledge about effective practice into preparation.

While documenting how standards have affected training and practice, Young and colleagues also noted that there are ways that the use of standards could be improved:

> From the perspective of program directors, state licensure and accreditation requirements are key levers for promoting program change, particularly in the areas of program mission, curriculum, and assessment. However, program directors did not agree that these sources of pressure were equally influential and beneficial. In fact, whereas accreditation review was identified by 78% of respondents as being influential, only 36% indicated that it was beneficial for promoting program quality. In contrast, 41% identified state licensure requirements as influencing program design, but 65% recognized it as a beneficial source of pressure.
>
> *(Young et al., 2016, p. 37)*

As we noted earlier, state policy has focused more on licensing requirements as drivers for change than on accreditation policy, and few states have yet to incorporate the program features most often identified by research as important, including strong clinical features, into their program-approval standards and processes (Anderson & Reynolds, 2015). A more recent study of seven states (Gates et al., 2020) notes that when such infusion has occurred, including through the use of both performance assessments for licensure and induction supports as in California, substantial change can be stimulated.

California's Overhaul of Principal Licensure

Licensure and accreditation changes in California that occurred between 2011 and 2017 integrated the new national standards and revised state standards for licensure in ways that emphasized educating diverse learners from a whole child perspective, integrating social and emotional learning and restorative practices, developing staff, using data, and involving stakehold-ers for school improvement. These administrator performance expectations were then translated into program-approval standards and new expectations for both preservice training and induction; later, they were translated into an administrator performance assessment, which was piloted for the first time in 2018–2019 (Reising et al., 2019).

These changes in expectations guiding program approval and induction were associated with changes in principals' perceptions of their preparation (Sutcher et al., 2017). Data from a representative sample of more than 400 California principals show that more recently prepared principals felt sig-nificantly better prepared than veteran principals in virtually all the areas that were integrated into the new standards, with very large changes in the ability to lead school improvement, especially for whole child approaches like social and emotional learning and restorative practices, and the ability to meet the needs of diverse learners. (See Table 6.3.) Newly graduated principals were also more likely to have experienced problem-based learn-ing approaches and field-based projects that were part of the new program

TABLE 6.3 California Principals' Reports of Preparation Experiences

Characteristics of Preparation	CA Veterans Completers (Before 2013)	CA Recent Completers (2013 or later)
Program Characteristics		
Problem-based learning approaches, such as action research or inquiry projects	69%⁻	78%
Field-based projects in which you applied ideas from your coursework to your experi-ence in the field	76%*	85%
A student cohort—a defined group of individ-uals who began the program together and stayed together throughout their courses	73%	80%
Instructional Leadership		
Develop students' higher-order thinking skills	54%**	73%
Raise schoolwide achievement on standard-ized tests	56%**	74%
Select effective curriculum strategies and materials	49%	58%
Lead instruction that supports implementa-tion of new state standards	47%**	64%
Leading and Managing School Improvement		
Use student and school data to inform con-tinuous school improvement	64%**	80%
Lead a schoolwide change process to improve student achievement	69%**	85%

Characteristics of Preparation	CA Veterans Completers (Before 2013)	CA Recent Completers (2013 or later)
Engage in self-improvement and your own continuous learning	71%**	87%
Create collegial and collaborative work environments	71%*	83%
Work with the school community, parents, educators, and other stakeholders	73%*	86%
Redesign a school's organization and structure to support deeper learning for teachers and students	63%	72%
Creating a Positive School Climate		
Lead schools that support students from diverse ethnic, racial, linguistic, and cultural backgrounds	70%*	82%
Lead schools that support students' social-emotional development	53%**	69%
Develop systems that meet children's needs and support their development in terms of physical and mental health	47%*	61%
Create a school environment that develops personally and socially responsible young people and uses discipline for restorative purposes	48%**	70%
Developing People		
Design professional learning opportunities for teachers and other staff	57%	65%
Help teachers improve through a cycle of observation and feedback	64%**	78%
Recruit and retain teachers and other staff	38%	40%
Manage school operations efficiently	63%	60%
Invest resources to support improvements in school performance	51%	60%
Meeting the Needs of All Learners		
Meet the needs of English learners	54%*	68%
Meet the needs of students with disabilities	53%**	75%
Equitably serve all children	62%**	79%

¯p < 0.10; ˚p < 0.05; ˚˚p < 0.01; ˚˚˚p < 0.001.

Note: Comparisons are made between principals who reported completing their preparation between 2013 and 2017, when the survey was fielded, and principals who had completed their preparation before 2013. Principals were asked, "To what extent did your leadership preparation program emphasize [*topic area*]?" Principals could select "not at all," "to a minimal extent," "somewhat," "to a moderate extent," or "to a great extent." The table shows the percentage of principals who selected "to a moderate extent" or "to a great extent."

Source: California Principal Survey (2017).

expectations, suggesting that the reforms did indeed affect program designs. As we found in our later study of California principals (see Chapter 4), the strength of preparation programs in these areas was, in turn, associated with principals' effectiveness.

The quality of internships in California also appears to be noticeably stronger than those in many other parts of the country (see Chapter 5). Of the 68% of California principals who reported having had an internship, the majority had more opportunities to take on administrative responsibilities (74% vs. 52% nationally) and felt their internships adequately prepared them for their first year as a principal (74% vs. 46% nationally).

Promising Examples of District Policy Influencing Practice

Throughout this section we have highlighted evidence about principal development policies that have influenced practice and outcomes in California, Illinois, North Carolina, and Pennsylvania. Like state policies, local district policies can influence principal development program design and implementation, which can influence principals' practice and school-level outcomes. Below we further highlight local policies that have made a difference.

Chicago Public Schools' Comprehensive Reforms

Chicago Public Schools (CPS), the nation's third-largest school system, has made a 25-year investment in school principal improvement policy that includes requiring all principal candidates to pass a district principal eligibility assessment, an innovation that required state legislation in 1996. In addition, for almost 20 years, Chicago has partnered with select university programs, such as those at the University of Illinois at Chicago (UIC) and Northeastern Illinois University, as well as with non-university-based programs, such as New Leaders, which provide intensive clinical training integrated into coursework focused on instructional leadership and school improvement.

During this time of intensive investment in principal preparation and development, CPS has steadily and dramatically improved its student performance measures, including its 3rd-grade reading scores and high-school graduation rates. From 2009 to 2014, CPS posted gains that translate to six years of academic growth in five years of elementary education. At the same time, the district narrowed and even reversed equity gaps with the rest of the state of Illinois (Reardon & Hinze-Pifer, 2017; Zavitkovsky & Tozer, 2017). Each of CPS's three largest enrollment groups—Latino/a, Black, and white—outperformed its statewide counterpart both below and above the free or reduced-price lunch mark on state and national achievement measures by 2017. Latino/a students, the largest enrollment group in CPS, surpassed the statewide scores for non-CPS white students on state and national assessments (Zavitkovsky & Tozer, 2017).

Observers of CPS's sustained academic improvements assert that the district's investment in school leadership policy is a contributing cause and that CPS's successes were influential in shaping state policy to reflect research findings in strong principal preparation (Rutledge & Tozer, 2019). Over 400 residency-trained principals from redesigned state- and CPS-approved programs have taken positions in CPS, and a disproportionate number of them have attained the highest positions in CPS administration, including, by 2022, the chief executive officer, chief education officer, chief of teaching and learning, and chief of early childhood education. (See also Chapter 2, where we report evidence from some of these programs.)

The Principal Pipeline Project

More rigorous examination of the outcomes of a set of similar initiatives in six large urban districts is available through two studies of the Principal Pipeline Initiative (PPI), funded by The Wallace Foundation. In 2011, these districts—Charlotte-Mecklenburg Schools, North Carolina; Denver Public Schools, Colorado; Gwinnett County Public Schools, Georgia; Hillsborough County Public Schools, Florida; New York City Department of Education, New York; and Prince George's County Public Schools, Maryland— set out to develop a principal pipeline strategy aimed at cultivating a steady supply of well-prepared and well-supported new principals. Though the program was implemented differently to fit local contexts, all districts shared the following common strategies:

- adopting standards of practice and performance that would guide principal preparation, hiring, evaluation, and support;
- delivering high-quality preservice preparation to high-potential candidates, typically through a combination of in-district programs and partnerships with university programs;
- using selective hiring and placement, informed by data on candidates' demonstrated skills, to match principal candidates to schools; and
- aligning on-the-job evaluation and support for novice principals with an enlarged role for principal supervisors in instructional leadership (Anderson & Turnbull, 2019).

The initiative is a useful example of what can be done at scale, as the districts are among the 50 largest school districts in the United States, each serving more than 80,000 students and operating more than 130 schools. The districts largely serve students from low-income families and between 65% and 96% students of color.

All six cities saw students in schools led by new principals in the initiative outperform those in comparison schools (Gates et al., 2019). After three or more years, schools with newly placed principals in PPI districts outperformed comparison schools with newly placed principals by 6% in reading and 3% in math. Newly placed principals in PPI districts were 6% more likely to remain in their schools for at least two years and were 8% more likely to remain in their schools for at least three years than newly placed principals in comparison schools—an important contributor to achievement effects, given that principal turnover is generally accompanied by an increase in teacher attrition and a decline in overall school achievement (Levin & Bradley, 2019). Effects were largest in elementary and middle schools and in schools in the lowest quartile of the achievement distribution. Across PPI districts, novice principals' ratings of their hiring, evaluation, and support experiences also improved between 2013 and 2015.

The reforms appear to work as a package (no single element accounts for the effects) and are viewed by the participating districts as affordable, at a cost of about $42 per pupil (about 0.5% of the districts' budgets) with strong returns on investment (Gates et al., 2019). Further, to date, the reforms appear sustainable. All six districts are maintaining principal pipelines, continuing to follow the vision of intentionally managing the career progressions of their aspiring principals and current principals. They continue to see principal standards as foundational in shaping the development and support of leaders through preparation programs, job descriptions, evaluation criteria, and coaching or mentoring. And as Anderson and Turnbull (2019) note, "District leaders made it clear that they see benefits from their principal pipelines, particularly in the strengths shown by recently appointed principals and in retention of these principals" (p. 6).

Summary of Principal Development Policy

Several recurring themes emerge from an examination of policy trends and from the limited set of studies that have examined policy outcomes.

First, standards for high-quality leadership practice have increasingly been integrated into local, state, and federal policies. A number of studies emphasized the power of standards to drive change when they are used coherently throughout the principal development system and are translated into tools such as performance assessments. Researchers of the PPI emphasized the relationship between state standards and local progress:

> State leader standards can provide a useful starting point for district efforts to develop clear, actionable leader standards. Several of the PPI districts

were able to leverage state leader standards in developing their own district standards and/or evaluation systems linked to those standards.

(Gates et al., 2019, p. 73)

The same point was made in case studies of program reforms driven by state policies (Young et al., 2016) and in a more recent implementation study of university program redesign as part of the PPI, in which state standards have played a significant role in curriculum redesign (Wang et al., 2018).

Second, while most states have integrated new standards into licensing and into accreditation and program-approval policies, fewer states have adopted the most high-leverage policies, like targeted recruitment of candidates, district participation in selection and program design, clinically rich internships that engage candidates in core leadership responsibilities with an expert mentor for an extended period of time, or performance-based assessments.

Third, a number of studies at both the state and local levels emphasize the importance of comprehensive, systemic change in which such high-leverage practices are adopted and linked to standards that influence recruitment, preparation, induction, and ongoing professional learning. Analysis of the PPI, for example, found that individual components of the districts' change agenda could not account for the gains in principal perceptions of their training and in student achievement:

Our analysis is consistent with the theory that comprehensive efforts to strategically implement pipeline activities across all components and align them with leader standards—which all districts did—are what matter. The component-by-component analysis found limited evidence that any one component or aspect of the pipeline efforts was associated with effects.

(Gates et al., 2019, p. 70)

As Manna (2021) outlines, successful principal pipelines are a product of state and local collaboration that involves standards that inform licensing and program approval as well as recruitment, preparation, professional development, and evaluation; high-quality preparation in partnerships that link theory to practice with strong practical applications; selective hiring and placement that value evidence of effectiveness from performance assessments; evaluation and support featuring aligned evaluation systems, alongside high-quality professional development and coaching; principal supervisors with tools and training for formative and summative support and evaluation; leader-tracking systems that identify and develop talent; and system supports that include funding, political support, and cross-district networks for shared learning.

States that have infused new principal preparation standards with strong field-based training and applied learning experiences (California, Illinois, and North Carolina) have shown increases in principals' perceptions of their preparedness and their likelihood of entering and staying in administrative jobs. Student learning gains and teacher effectiveness increases were associated with Pennsylvania's statewide induction program that combined mentoring with intensive professional development featuring a long-term project supporting instructional improvement.

Finally, while there has been some progress since 2000 in principals' access to important learning opportunities, there is still a long way to go. Less than 60% of principals nationally report that they received preservice preparation for their jobs, and just over 50% have said they received mentoring or coaching—one of the most important aspects of learning that improves principals' effectiveness.

Given the results of our literature review and policy scan, it is clear that more research is needed on the outcomes of efforts in jurisdictions that have invested in high-leverage policies, as well as research on the state policies associated with more access to professional learning in key areas using productive learning strategies, such as applied learning opportunities, internships, coaching and mentoring, and principal networks.

7
RESEARCH AND POLICY IMPLICATIONS

Research has shown clearly that strong school leadership is critical for shaping positive learning environments, supporting high-quality teachers and teaching, and influencing student outcomes. There is a growing knowledge base about principal learning opportunities that foster principals' abilities to support these conditions in schools. Major changes in policies have also altered the principal learning landscape.

This report combines current knowledge from the research literature and our own analyses to better understand the elements of high-quality programs that have been associated with positive principal, teacher, and student outcomes, ranging from principals' feelings of preparedness and their engagement in more effective practices to stronger teacher retention and improved student achievement. It also examines the extent to which principals have opportunities to participate in programs with those elements and the policies that drive both the development of high-quality programs and access to them. In this concluding section, we summarize key findings and discuss implications of this research for researchers and policymakers.

Summary

A growing body of literature indicates that high-quality principal preparation and professional development programs are associated with positive principal, teacher, and student outcomes. Many programs have adopted the practices of exemplary leadership programs identified in *Preparing Leaders for a Changing World*, including proactive recruitment; meaningful and authentic learning opportunities that apply learning in practice;

DOI: 10.4324/9781003380450-7

a focus on leading instruction, developing people, creating a collaborative learning organization, and managing change; mentoring or coaching, along with feedback and opportunities for reflection; and cohort or networking structures that create a professional learning community. Growing research illustrates how principal learning programs that reflect these elements contribute to the development of principals' leadership knowledge and skills as well as to positive teacher outcomes and increased student achievement.

Recent studies especially reinforce the importance of field-based internships and problem-based learning opportunities. Through these opportunities, principals can actualize the theories they learn in coursework and practice the many skills and tasks required of today's principals. The efficacy of these opportunities is enhanced when they include an experienced, expert mentor or coach who can provide support and guidance to novice or experienced principals.

Recent literature has also explored programs designed to help principals meet the needs of diverse learners. This topic is particularly salient given the increasingly diverse student population in the United States, the growing attention to equity concerns, and research showing the importance of culturally responsive practices and individualized supports. Recent studies suggest that, through applied learning opportunities (e.g., action research, field-based projects) and reflective projects (e.g., cultural autobiographies, cross-cultural interviews, and analytic journals), aspiring principals can deepen their understanding of the ways in which biases associated with race, class, language, disability, and other factors manifest in society and schools and how educators can work toward more equitable opportunities and outcomes.

Access to important content in preservice preparation and professional development has been increasing for principals, but access to powerful learning strategies, such as applied learning, internships, mentoring, and coaching, is much lower. Our analyses of principal surveys found that most principals reported having at least minimal access to important content related to leading instruction, managing change, developing people, shaping a positive school culture, and meeting the needs of diverse learners, and access to this content has increased over time. Principals who were certified in the past ten years were more likely to report access to this content and to comprehensive preparation than earlier-certified principals. Even with these improvements, a minority of principals nationally reported having had access to the authentic, job-based learning opportunities that the research has identified as being important to their development. Only 46% of all principals reported having an internship that allowed them to take on real leadership responsibilities characteristic of a high-quality internship experience. And very few principals reported having access to coaching or mentoring, despite the research showing the strong importance of these types of supports.

Access to high-quality preparation and professional development differs across states and communities. Compared to principals nationally, a greater percentage of California principals reported that they had access to preparation and professional development in nearly every important content area, and a greater percentage reported that they had authentic, job-based learning opportunities in both pre- and in-service contexts. At the same time, North Carolina principals reported having far less access to nearly every kind of professional development, as budgets have been severely cut in that state.

Access to high-quality preparation also varies by school poverty level within states and nationally. Principals in low-poverty schools were much more likely than principals in high-poverty schools to report that they had learning opportunities in a number of important areas, and they were more likely to report that they experienced problem-based and cohort-based preparation. This disparity, however, did not appear among California principals—large majorities of principals in all kinds of schools had access to professional learning, suggesting that policy can influence the availability and distribution of these opportunities.

Across the country, most principals reported wanting more professional development in nearly all topics, but they also reported obstacles in pursuing learning opportunities, including a lack of time and money.

Policies that support high-quality principal learning programs can make a difference in states and districts that have overhauled standards and have used them to inform preparation, clinically rich learning opportunities, and assessment, the evidence suggests that the quality of principal learning has improved. More state and local policymakers have adopted standards for principal licensing and program accreditation. These are important levers for improvement if they are infused throughout the relevant learning, supervision, and assessment systems. However, few states adopted other high-leverage policies, such as requiring a rigorous selection process, a clinically rich internship, district-university partnerships, or a performance-based assessment for licensure.

All states planned to bolster their efforts to support leadership development through the Every Student Succeeds Act (ESSA), using aspects of the law to strengthen preparation, reimagine on-the-job support, advance equity-focused leadership, distribute leaders more equitably, and build leadership pipelines.

Evidence from several states and districts shows that where leadership policies and implementation are strong, access to high-quality principal learning opportunities increases. In some cases, well-implemented policies have translated into stronger student achievement, such as Chicago's investments in new forms of initial preparation for principals, Pennsylvania's induction program for new principals, and six districts' engagements in a Principal Pipeline Initiative for career-long learning.

Research Implications

Our research syntheses in chapters 2 and 3—"Principal Preparation" and "Principal Professional Development"—describe the growing bodies of research that address questions about the features and outcomes of high-quality principal preparation and professional development. At the same time, the syntheses reveal gaps in the available research and methodological weaknesses. Our recommendations for future research include the following.

Broaden the scope of research to include stronger descriptions of program content as well as pedagogical approaches. As a whole, the current research on principal learning opportunities focuses heavily on the structures for principal learning (for example, workshops, coaching, clinical experiences). This research has been instructive in suggesting the importance of providing aspiring principals with opportunities for quality internships under the tutelage of experienced mentors and providing current principals with coaching and mentoring. It has also shown how aspiring and current principals benefit from applied learning opportunities in which they engage in problem-based learning and field-based projects to apply their learning to authentic school-based situations.

Recent research, however, has focused less extensively on the content of principals' learning. To what extent and in what ways are principals gaining the knowledge, skills, and dispositions they need to be successful? To what extent are they able to set a clear vision and direction, engage in instructionally focused interactions with teachers that attend to the needs of diverse learners, build a productive school climate, facilitate collaboration and professional learning communities, manage personnel and resources strategically, and manage change and school improvement (Grissom et al., 2021; Leithwood & Louis, 2012)?

Likewise, in what ways can principals learn to meet the needs of diverse learners? Systemic racial and economic inequities plague the education system and are deeply rooted in our history and policies (George & Darling-Hammond, 2019). Principals can counteract the harms of discrimination by creating learning environments that are equitable and racially just, that foster culturally responsive practices, and that recognize student diversity as an asset (Cosner et al., 2015; Darling-Hammond & Cook-Harvey, 2018). While there is emerging literature on preparing principals to serve diverse learners, there is only scant attention to this content in the literature on professional development.

To broaden the field's knowledge about high-quality principal preparation and professional development, future research can examine the content as well as the pedagogy in emerging programs and the extent to which these address the development of important leadership skills. It would be useful for major survey efforts such as the National Teacher and Principal Surveys (previously called the Schools and Staffing Surveys) to include a constant set of survey items on the content of preparation and professional development, much like those featured in our surveys, so that trends can be seen over time and across states and regions. Documenting outcomes associated with particular kinds of preparation and professional development efforts will also be important.

Account for principals' prior experiences, program recruitment and selection criteria, and district contexts. The current research on principal preparation and professional development rarely takes into account the background or characteristics of program participants. However, research indicates that the backgrounds and experiences of principals, including their prior effectiveness as teachers, are related to their effectiveness as principals (see, for example, Goldhaber et al., 2019). Further, a program's candidate pool is directly related to its recruitment and selection criteria (Wechsler & Wojcikiewicz, 2023). As earlier research found, a common feature of exemplary professional development is vigorous, targeted recruitment and selection of dynamic teachers who are instructional leaders (Darling-Hammond et al., 2007).

Similarly, there is an emerging literature on the value of teachers of color to the achievement of students of color (Carver-Thomas, 2018) and the value of principals of color—and others who offer targeted supports—to the retention of teachers of color (Campoli, 2017). Both the recruitment of candidates and the design and outcomes of professional learning experiences will be shaped by what candidates already know and believe from their personal experience and their teaching experience when they enter. Yet few research studies attend to the characteristics and experiences of program participants or programs' method of selection.

What are the interactions between a professional learning strategy and the pathways to the role of the principalship and principals' prior knowledge and experiences? For example, one randomized controlled trial found that an effort to teach principals how to give teachers evaluative feedback was successful with experienced principals and those with stronger mentors—whose students experienced learning gains—but unsuccessful with most novice principals, who were rated more negatively by teachers over the course of the project and were unable to support student learning gains (Herrmann et al., 2019). What kinds of knowledge and skills do principals need to become good instructional leaders? How might that interact with their prior knowledge and experience? And how might these understandings guide both recruitment and program design? These are the kinds of questions researchers could plumb more deeply to support program success.

The context, too, varies considerably across districts, not only in terms of resources and student demographics but also in important policies that affect what principals are able to do and how they can enact the new knowledge and skills they acquire in preparation and professional development (Wechsler & Wojcikiewicz, 2023). If principal mobility is high or if principals are required to enforce the use of less effective instructional strategies, the potential positive effects of a principal development program may not be realized.

Future research can explore the differences that aspiring and current principals bring to their preservice and in-service programs (e.g., years of successful experience in teaching, mentoring, or administrative roles; racial/ethnic background and family experiences; bilingualism) and how their backgrounds affect their experiences with and the outcomes of preparation and professional development. It can also attend to how program elements, such as recruitment and selection processes, and district policies and practices impact who is participating in principal learning programs and how principals are able to employ their new knowledge and skills.

Better define outcome measures, and include a broader spectrum of outcomes. As previously described, research has identified a range of skills principals need to effect positive outcomes in their schools. For example, effective principals engage in instructionally focused interactions with teachers through their feedback and coaching; support for professional development and professional learning communities; engagement in collaborative decision-making and planning time; teacher evaluations; and engagement in schoolwide planning and change. They manage personnel and resources strategically through hiring, staff assignments and placements, and attention to teacher retention (Grissom et al., 2021). Yet much of the current research on principal preparation and professional development tends to focus on broad, ill-defined measures, such as principals' "readiness to lead" or their "leadership abilities."

Future research can address more specific outcomes and measure them in multiple ways. For example, in addition to asking aspiring principals and current principals if they feel prepared or better equipped to lead in general, studies can focus more explicitly on principals' attainment of the important leadership skills. Researchers could ask, what kinds of feedback and support do principals give to teachers, and with what effects? What strategies do principals enact to retain teachers? Also, rather than merely asking principals in surveys or interviews what their perceptions are of their knowledge and skills, researchers can examine actual practice through observations, document review, or other such means. Researchers could ask those who work directly with the principal about the knowledge and skills they observe, especially those who have observed principals before and after their participation in professional learning opportunities, including teachers; other school staff; students; district leadership; and coaches, mentors, and supervisors.

Relatedly, a new body of research shows that principals can impact student achievement, teacher retention, and other school outcomes, such as student attendance and exclusionary discipline (Grissom et al., 2021). The ways in which these outcomes are achieved deserves study, as do those related to teacher retention, instructional practices, and collaboration. Further, research can broaden measures related to students beyond achievement to include graduation and attendance rates, students' sense of belonging, and students' social-emotional well-being, examining how principals' learning opportunities are associated with their practices and student outcomes.

Take a longitudinal view.

Many current studies look at outcomes only once, generally right after a specific class or program. However, we know from other research that it often takes about three years for a principal's effect to become measurable in terms of school-level changes (Pham et al., 2018). Future research should seek, whenever possible, to measure program outcomes over time. Doing so not only will allow potential effects to become visible but will also provide a better understanding of the mechanisms by which principals' knowledge and skills translate into behaviors and practices and then into influences on staff and students.

Pay attention to how programs are implemented.

Another important consideration in examining the features of high-quality principal learning opportunities and their outcomes is the extent to which the program was implemented as intended. Simply looking at outcomes may result in inaccurate interpretations of the findings. Although most studies of principal preparation and in-service professional development describe the program studied, including various program components and expectations for participants, fewer studies delve deeply into the integrity of the program's implementation. Program integrity relies on adherence to the program plan, including whether the dosage (i.e., the amount of time and treatment provided) matches the program design; the quality of program delivery; and engagement of participants (e.g., whether participants attend the sessions and complete assignments). Knowledge of the extent to which program implementation varies on any of these dimensions can inform our understanding of study findings and might also point to the feasibility of the program to be implemented as intended.

Use mixed methods skillfully to deepen the understanding of program processes and their effects, especially those that link program features to outcomes. Finally, most of the current research uses descriptive methodologies and relies on surveys and interviews with participants or graduates of a single program. While some studies use comparison groups and correlational analyses, very few studies use randomized controlled trials, quasi-experimental designs, or other designs that use controls. And those that do often fail to fully describe the program under study, the nature of its implementation, or the nature of the comparison group, which means that findings can be misinterpreted or uninterpretable.

Future research can employ a wider range of methodologies and can employ chosen methodologies more carefully. For example, experimental or quasi-experimental designs, if properly designed and conducted with sufficient information about the program, its implementation, and the comparison group's experiences, could strengthen researchers' ability to make causal claims about preparation or in-service programs and to contribute useful information to program selection and development. In-depth case studies that extend over time and combine interviews, close observations of practices, and surveys of participants and staff with outcome data could provide the details about what programs offer and how they develop principals' knowledge and skills.

Policy Implications

Because of the importance of strong principals for student achievement and teaching quality and because state and local policies are important levers in improving the quality of principal learning, policymakers have good reason to invest in the preparation and ongoing professional development of principals. Our analyses of high-quality principal learning programs and the policies that foster such programs inform the following policy recommendations.

Develop and better use state licensing and program approval standards to support high-quality principal preparation and development.
Over the past two decades, many states have developed policies that align with the research on effective principal development. All states and Washington, DC, have adopted standards to guide principal licensure, and many have developed new requirements for principals, such as having a valid educator license, experience in an educational setting, completion of a preparation program, and passage of an assessment. Yet only a few states have fully used the standards to guide performance-based approaches to licensing or intensive approaches to preparation program approval that would result in stronger program models. Likewise, only a few states have adopted high-leverage program-approval policies, such as requiring clinically rich internships and university-district partnerships that support proactive recruitment. Because policy shifts have not taken on the most critical strategies in the most powerful ways, considerable variability still exists in terms of principals' opportunities for high-quality preservice learning across the country.

The stronger use of licensure and program-approval standards can help ensure that programs include the features of high-quality programs identified in this book. They can help align the content of professional learning opportunities with the knowledge principals need to produce positive school outcomes, such as leading instruction, shaping a positive school culture, and developing people. Importantly, they can also focus on meeting the needs of diverse learners, creating inclusive and supportive environments, and fostering learning environments that support whole child development.

The structure of professional learning opportunities is also critically important, and standards—as well as their implementation in program approval—can emphasize the types of opportunities that matter according to the research. Especially important are quality internships for aspiring principals and applied learning opportunities accompanied by coaching and mentoring for practicing principals under the auspices of an experienced, expert principal. These opportunities typically require investments as well from the state and/or the district.

It is important that standards be uniformly applied to all programs once they are adopted. As Manna (2021) notes, it may be helpful for state policy to allow a variety of providers, so long as they implement programs held to demanding standards. "In contrast," he notes, "state policy that incorporates alternative programs which could allow providers to . . . deviat(e) from high-quality state standards, runs the risk of approving weaker pre-service preparation routes" (p. 15), which has long-term negative consequences for candidates and the field.

Invest in a statewide infrastructure for principal professional learning. ESSA provides federal funds that states can leverage to support the development of school leaders. ESSA permits states to set aside 3% of their Title II formula funds to strengthen the quality of school leaders, including by investing in principal recruitment, preparation, induction, and development. In addition, states can leverage other funds under Titles I and II of ESSA to invest in school leadership as a means to strengthen both teacher and school-leader quality and, ultimately, to improve schools. These funds were dramatically expanded by the American Rescue Plan Act of 2021 and can be used to prepare principals to support students' social-emotional and learning needs during and beyond the COVID-19 pandemic.

Using ESSA funds and other investments, states are in a position to ensure principals have coordinated, high-quality, and sustained professional learning. Financial support is essential because it makes possible the features of high-quality programming, including continuity in learning opportunities and robust clinical experiences. Leadership academies can provide some of this deep, coherent training, along with training and support for mentors and coaches who work with leaders over time. Paid internships for leadership preparation, like those offered in Illinois and North Carolina, can enable high-quality candidates to enter school leadership without going into debt. They also make it feasible for candidates to take the necessary time for intensive clinical placements. Support for clinical partnerships between programs and districts can ensure that internships, along with mentoring opportunities for novice principals and coaching for veterans, become universal and sustainable.

Encourage greater attention to equity. Surveys of principals nationally and in North Carolina reveal that principals' access to high-quality learning opportunities varies by school poverty level. Principals in low-poverty schools were much more likely than principals in high-poverty schools to report that they had learning opportunities in a number of content areas associated with effective leadership, and they were more likely to report that they experienced problem-based and cohort-based preparation. Improving the quality of principal learning programs and increasing access for all principals across settings to access high-quality programs would be especially beneficial to children who are currently furthest from opportunity. This can be done by directing professional development resources to those schools or districts and by offering funding to underwrite high-quality preparation for prospective principals who will work in those schools.

Programs, too, can include more content and applied learning opportunities that focus on issues of equity and culturally responsive leadership. The principal preparation research has shown that a specific focus on equity-oriented leadership has the potential to develop aspiring principals' knowledge and skills for meeting the needs of diverse learners. We found less focus on this issue with respect to in-service professional development, however. Both preparation and professional development programs can purposefully build principals' knowledge, for example, to foster equitable school environments, deploy resources equitably, support culturally responsive curriculum, create welcoming and authentic partnerships with families, and develop hiring and induction policies that support a diverse teacher workforce.

Undertake comprehensive policy reforms at the local level to build a robust pipeline of qualified school principals and a coherent system of development.

Encourage districts, through competitive grants and/or technical assistance, to launch pipeline programs such as those described in this report that have proven effective at finding teachers with leadership potential and carrying them along a pathway to becoming a principal. Pipelines for leadership candidates start before preparation with the targeted recruitment of qualified candidates. Deliberate and dynamic recruitment can identify teachers who have the potential and dispositions to engage in the leadership behaviors that research has shown to be important for producing school outcomes. It also gives schools and districts the opportunity to pick candidates who will meet their local needs, who are known to be dynamic teachers and instructional leaders, and who better represent historically underserved populations.

Following recruitment, pipelines incentivize and support ongoing learning for leaders, starting with preparation and induction and running through high-quality, shared learning opportunities for veteran leaders. Pipelines help keep strong principals engaged and build local capacity. They also contribute to the capacity of schools and districts by creating opportunities for collaboration between leaders in the pipeline and other staff, such as mentor principals and principal supervisors engaged in supporting the different aspects of the pipeline. In these ways, pipelines not only improve the practice of individuals and create a supply of qualified leaders for school and district positions, but they also contribute to coherence in practice that supports systemic change and increased student learning.

Conclusion

Looking across all the evidence, we conclude that comprehensive principal preparation and professional development programs are positively associated with benefits for principals, teachers, and students. Especially important are clinical experiences, mentoring, and applied learning opportunities. However, few principals have had access to the kinds of comprehensive programs or learning structures that support their success, and access is variable across states due to differences in policies and available resources. Policy shifts appear to influence outcomes, and there is much that states and districts can do to foster and support high-quality principal learning. The field has moved a great deal over the past two decades, embracing many of the lessons identified in *Preparing Leaders for a Changing World*, but there is still a great distance to go to ensure that all principals get access to the kind of learning opportunities that will allow them to support all children's learning and well-being. Moving forward, improved research can continue to build the field's knowledge about how to best develop high-quality principals, and enhanced policies can create a principal learning system that, as a whole, will better serve principals, the staff they support, and, ultimately, all children.

REFERENCES

Adams, J. E., & Copland, M. A. (2005). *When learning counts: Rethinking licenses for school leaders.* Center on Reinventing Public Education.

Alsbury, T. L., & Hackmann, D. G. (2006). Learning from experience: Initial findings of a mentoring/induction program for novice principals and superintendents. *Planning and Changing, 37,* 169–189.

Alvin Ailey American Dance Theatre. *AileyCamp.* https://www.alvinailey.org/about/arts-education-community-programs/aileycamp

Anderson, E., & Reynolds, A. L. (2015). The state of state policies for principal preparation program approval and candidate licensure. *Journal of Research on Leadership Education, 10*(3), 193–221. https://doi.org/10.1177/1942775115614292

Anderson, L. M., & Turnbull, B. J. (2019). *Sustaining a principal pipeline.* Policy Studies Associates. https://www.wallacefoundation.org/knowledge-center/Documents/Sustaining-a-Principal-Pipeline.pdf

Augustine, C. H., Gonzalez, G., Ikemoto Schuyler, G., Russell, J., Zellman, G. L., Constant, L., Armstrong, J., & Dembosky, J. W. (2009). *Improving school leadership: The promise of cohesive leadership systems.* RAND Corporation.

Augustine-Shaw, D., & Liang, J. (2016). Embracing new realities: Professional growth for new principals and mentors. *Educational Considerations, 43*(3), 10–17. https://doi.org/10.4148/0146-9282.1016

Ballenger, J., Alford, B., McCune, S., & McCune, D. (2009). Obtaining validation from graduates on a restructured principal preparation program. *Journal of School Leadership, 19*(5), 533–558. https://doi.org/10.1177/105268460901900502

Barnes, C. A., Camburn, E., Sanders, B. R., & Sebastian, J. (2010). Developing instructional leaders: Using mixed methods to explore the black box of planned change in principals' professional practice. *Educational Administration Quarterly, 46*(2), 241. https://doi.org/10.1177/1094670510361748

Bartanen, B. (2020). Principal quality and student attendance. *Educational Researcher, 49*(2), 101–113. https://doi.org/10.3102/0013189X19898702

Bartee, R. D. (2012). Recontextualizing the knowledge and skill involved with redesigned principal preparation: Implications of cultural and social capital in teaching, learning, and leading for administrators. *Planning and Changing*, *43*(3–4), 322.

Bastian, K. C., & Fuller, S. C. (2016). *The North Carolina Principal Fellows Program: A comprehensive evaluation*. University of North Carolina at Chapel Hill Education Policy Initiative at Carolina.

Batagiannis, S. C. (2011). Promise and possibility for aspiring principals: An emerging leadership identity through learning to do action research. *The Qualitative Report*, *16*(5), 1304–1329. https://doi.org/10.46743/2160-3715/2011.1300

Beard, K. S. (2018). Toward a theory of engaged school leadership: Positive psychology and principal candidates' sense of engagement and their preparedness to lead engagement. *Journal of School Leadership*, *28*(6), 742–771. https://doi.org/10.1177/105268461802800603

Bengtson, E., Airola, D., Peer, D., & Davis, D. (2012). Using peer learning support networks and reflective practice: The Arkansas leadership academy master principal program. *International Journal of Educational Leadership Preparation*, *7*(3).

Berry, B., Bastian, K. C., Darling-Hammond, L., & Kini, T. (2019). *How teaching and learning conditions affect teacher retention and school performance in North Carolina*. Learning Policy Institute. https://learningpolicyinstitute.org/sites/default/files/product-files/Leandro_Working_Conditions_REPORT.pdf

Béteille, T., Kalogrides, D., & Loeb, S. (2012). Stepping stones: Principal career paths and school outcomes. *Social Science Research*, *41*(4), 904–919. https://doi.org/10.1016/j.ssresearch.2012.03.003

Bonilla-Silva, E. (2017). *Racism without racists: Color-blind racism and the persistence of racial inequality in America*. Rowman & Littlefield.

Borden, A. M., Preskill, S. L., & DeMoss, K. (2012). A new turn toward learning for leadership: Findings from an exploratory coursework pilot project. *Journal of Research on Leadership Education*, *7*(1), 123–152. https://doi.org/10.1177/1942775112443929

Boren, D. M., & Hallam, P. R. (2019). Examining a university-multiple district sponsored academy from the perspective of principal supervisors. *AASA Journal of Scholarship & Practice*, *16*(1), 4. https://link.gale.com/apps/doc/A587261719/AONE?u=anon~cbfd044a&sid=googleScholar&xid=6a28be2c

Boren, D. M., Hallam, P. R., Ray, N. C., Gill, C. L., & Li, K. (2017). Examining effective principal professional development through a university-district sponsored principals academy. *Educational Practice and Theory*, *39*(2), 87–106. https://doi.org/10.7459/ept/39.2.06

Braun, D., Billups, F. D., & Gable, R. K. (2013). Transforming equity-oriented leaders: Principal residency network program evaluation. *NCPEA Education Leadership Review*, *14*(1), 161–181. https://files.eric.ed.gov/fulltext/EJ1012950.pdf

Brody, J. L., Vissa, J., & Weathers, J. M. (2010). School leader professional socialization: The contribution of focused observations. *Journal of Research on Leadership Education*, *5*(14), 611–651. https://doi.org/10.1177/194277511000501401

Brown, K. M. (2005). Social justice education for preservice leaders: Evaluating transformative learning strategies. *Equity & Excellence in Education*, *38*(2), 155–167. https://doi.org/10.1080/10665680590935133

Camburn, E. M., Goldring, E., Sebastian, J., May, H., & Huff, J. (2016). An examination of the benefits, limitations, and challenges of conducting randomized experiments with principals. *Educational Administration Quarterly, 52*(2), 187–220. https://doi.org/10.1177/0013161X15617808

Campoli, A. K. (2017). Supportive principals and black teacher turnover: ESSA as an opportunity to improve retention. *Journal of School Leadership, 27,* 675–700.

Campoli, A. K., & Darling-Hammond, L. (with Levin, S., & Podolsky, A.). (2022). *Principal learning opportunities and school outcomes: Evidence from California.* Learning Policy Institute.

Carraway, J., & Young, T. (2015). Implementation of a districtwide policy to improve principals' instructional leadership: Principals' sensemaking of the skillful observation and coaching laboratory. *Educational Policy, 29*(1), 230–256. https://doi.org/10.1177/0895904814564216

Carver-Thomas, D. (2018). *Diversifying the teaching profession: How to recruit and retain teachers of color.* Learning Policy Institute. https://doi.org/10.54300/559.310.

Carver-Thomas, D., & Darling-Hammond, L. (2017). *Teacher turnover: Why it matters and what we can do about it.* Learning Policy Institute. https://learningpolicyinstitute.org/product/teacher-turnover-report

Casey, P. J., Starrett, T. M., & Dunlap, K. (2013). Residual effects of a professional development project for aspiring school leaders. *Academy of Educational Leadership Journal, 17*(2), 81–93.

Castro, J. I. (2004). Promoting leadership development and collaboration in rural schools. In J. H. Chrispeels (Ed.), *Learning to lead together: The promise and challenge of sharing leadership* (pp. 327–341). SAGE Publications, Inc. https://doi.org/10.4135/9781452232416.n13

Clark, D., Martorell, P., & Rockoff, J. (2009). *School principals and school performance* (Working Paper No. 38). CALDER, The Urban Institute.

Clayton, J. K., Sanzo, K. L., & Myran, S. (2013). Understanding mentoring in leadership development: Perspectives of district administrators and aspiring leaders. *Journal of Research on Leadership Education, 8*(1), 77–96. https://doi.org/10.1177/1942775112464959

Coelli, M., & Green, D. A. (2012). Leadership effects: School principals and student outcomes. *Economics of Education Review, 31*(1), 92–109. https://doi.org/10.1016/j.econedurev.2011.09.001

Coggshall, J. (2015). *Title II, part A: Don't scrap it, don't dilute it, fix it.* American Institutes for Research. https://www.air.org/resource/brief-title-ii-part-dont-scrap-it-dont-dilute-it-fix-it

Copland, M. A. (2000). Problem-based learning and prospective principals' problem-framing ability. *Educational Administration Quarterly, 36*(4), 585–607. https://doi.org/10.1177/00131610021969119

Corcoran, R. P. (2017). Preparing principals to improve student achievement. *Child & Youth Care Forum, 46*(5), 769–781. https://doi.org/10.1007/s10566-017-9399-9

Corcoran, S. P., Schwartz, A. E., & Weinstein, M. (2012). Training your own: The impact of New York City's Aspiring Principals Program on student achievement. *Educational Evaluation and Policy Analysis, 34*(2), 232–253. https://doi.org/10.3102/0162373712437206

Cosner, S., De Voto, C., & Rah'man, A. (2018). Drawing in the school context as a learning resource in school leader development: Application-oriented projects in active learning designs. *Journal of Research on Leadership Education, 13*(3), 238–255. https://doi.org/10.1177/1942775118763872

Cosner, S., Tozer, S., & Smylie, M. (2012). The Ed.D. program at the University of Illinois at Chicago: Using continuous improvement to promote school leadership preparation. *Planning and Changing, 43*(1–2), 127. https://files.eric.ed.gov/fulltext/EJ977551.pdf

Cosner, S., Tozer, S., Zavitkovsky, P., & Whalen, S. P. (2015). Cultivating exemplary school leadership preparation at a research intensive university. *Journal of Research on Leadership Education, 10*(1), 11–38. https://doi.org/10.1177/1942775115569575

Darling-Hammond, L. (2019). *Investing in student success: Lessons from state school finance reforms.* Learning Policy Institute. https://learningpolicyinstitute.org/product/investing-student-success-school-finance-reforms-report

Darling-Hammond, L., Bastian, K., Berry, B., Carver-Thomas, D., Kini, T., Levin, S., & McDiarmid, W. (2019). *Educator supply, demand, and quality in North Carolina: Current status and recommendations.* Learning Policy Institute. https://learningpolicyinstitute.org/product/leandro-educator-supply-demand-brief

Darling-Hammond, L., & Cook-Harvey, C. M. (2018). *Educating the whole child: Improving school climate to support student success.* Learning Policy Institute. https://doi.org/10.54300/145.655

Darling-Hammond, L., Flook, L., Cook-Harvey, C., Barron, B., & Osher, D. (2020). Implications for educational practice of the science of learning and development. *Applied Developmental Science, 24*(2), 97–140. https://doi.org/10.1080/10888691.2018.1537791

Darling-Hammond, L., LaPointe, M., Meyerson, D., Orr, M. T., & Cohen, C. (2007). *Preparing school leaders for a changing world: Lessons from exemplary leadership development programs.* Stanford University, Stanford Educational Leadership Institute. https://www.wallacefoundation.org/knowledge-center/Documents/Preparing-School-Leaders.pdf

Darling-Hammond, L., & Oakes, J. (2019). *Preparing teachers for deeper learning.* Harvard Education Press.

De Voto, C., & Reedy, M. A. (2019). Are states under ESSA prioritizing education leadership to improve schools? *Journal of Research on Leadership Education, 16*(3), 175–199. https://doi.org/10.1177/1942775119890637

Della Sala, M. R., Klar, H. W., Lindle, J. C., Reese, K. L., Knoeppel, R. C., Campbell, M., & Buskey, F. C. (2013). Implementing a cross-district principal mentoring program: A human resources approach to developing midcareer principals' leadership capacities. *Journal of School Public Relations, 34*(4), 162–192. https://doi.org/10.3138/jspr.34.2.162

DeMoss, K., Wood, C., & Howell, R. (2007). Eliminating isolation to foster learner-centered leadership: Lessons from rural schools and research universities. In A. B. Danzig, K. M. Borman, B. A. Jones, & W. F. Wright (Eds.), *Learner-centered leadership: Research, policy, and practice* (pp. 149–170). https://doi.org/10.4324/9781315091945-7

Dodson, R. L. (2014). Which field experiences best prepare future school leaders? An analysis of Kentucky's principal preparation program. *Educational Research Quarterly, 37*(4), 41–56. https://files.eric.ed.gov/fulltext/EJ1061927.pdf

Dodson, R. L. (2015). What makes them the best? An analysis of the relationship between state education quality and principal preparation practices. *International Journal of Education Policy & Leadership, 10*(7), 1–21. https://doi.org/10.22230/ijepl.2015v10n7a634

Donmoyer, R., Yennie-Donmoyer, J., & Galloway, F. (2012). The search for connections across principal preparation, principal performance, and student achievement in an exemplary principal preparation program. *Journal of Research on Leadership Education, 7*(1), 5–43. https://doi.org/10.1177/1942775112440631

Duncan, H. E., & Stock, M. J. (2010). Mentoring and coaching rural school leaders: What do they need? *Mentoring & Tutoring: Partnership in Learning, 18*(3), 293–311. https://doi.org/10.1080/13611267.2010.492947

Ermeling, B., Tatsui, T., & Young, K. (2015). Virtual coaching for instructional leaders: A multi-method investigation of technology-enabled external assistance. *Teachers College Record, 117*(11). https://doi.org/10.1177/016146811511701108

Finn, C. E., Broad, E., Meyer, L., & Feistritzer, E. (2003). *Better leaders for America's schools: A manifesto.* Fordham Institute; The Broad Foundation. https://fordhinstitute.org/national/research/better-leaders-americas-schools-manifesto

Friedland, H. A. (2005). Leading leaders: Lessons from the field. *Academic Exchange Quarterly, 9*(2), 109–114.

Gates, S. M., Baird, M.D., Master, B.K., & Chavez-Herrerias, E.R. (2019). *Principal Pipelines: A Feasible, Affordable, and Effective Way for Districts to Improve Schools.* Santa Monica, CA: RAND Corporation. https://www.rand.org/pubs/research_reports/RR2666.html.

Gates, S. M., Hamilton, L. S., Martorell, P., Burkhauser, S., Heaton, P., Pierson, A., Baird, M., Vuollo, M., Li, J. J., Lavery, D. C., Harvey, M., & Gu, K. (2014). *Preparing principals to raise student achievement: Implementation and effects of the New Leaders program in ten districts.* RAND Corporation. https://doi.org/10.7249/RR507

Gates, S. M., Woo, A., Xenakis, L., Wang, E. L., Herman, R., Andrew, M., & Todd, I. (2020). *Using state-level policy levers to promote principal quality: Lessons from seven states partnering with principal preparation programs and districts.* RAND Corporation. https://doi.org/10.7249/RRA413-1

George, J., & Darling-Hammond, L. (2019). *The federal role and school integration: Brown's promise and present challenges.* Learning Policy Institute. https://learningpolicyinstitute.org/product/federal-role-school-integration-browns-promise-report

George W. Bush Institute, & American Institutes for Research. (2016, October). *Following the leaders: An analysis of graduate effectiveness from five principal preparation programs.* George W. Bush Institute. https://gwbcenter.imgix.net/Resources/gwbi-grad-effectiveness-principal-prep.pdf

Gilbert, K. A. (2017). Innovative leadership preparation: Enhancing legal literacy to create 21st century ready principals. *Academy of Educational Leadership Journal, 21*(1), 1–17. https://files.eric.ed.gov/fulltext/EJ875408.pdf

Goff, P., Guthrie, J. E., Goldring, E., & Bickman, L. (2014). Changing principals' leadership through feedback and coaching. *Journal of Educational Administration, 52*(5), 682–704. https://doi.org/10.1108/JEA-10-2013-0113

Goldhaber, D., Holden, K., & Chen, B. (2019). *Do more effective teachers become more effective principals?* (Working Paper No. 215-0119-1). CALDER. https://files.eric.ed.gov/fulltext/ED600819.pdf

Goldrick, L. (2016). *Support from the start: A 50-state review of policies on new educator induction and mentoring.* New Teacher Center. http://68.77.48.18/RandD/Other/50-State%20Review%20of%20New%20Teacher%20Induction%20-%20NTC.pdf

Goldring, E. B., Rubin, M., & Herrmann, M. (2021). *The role of assistant principals: Evidence and insights for advancing school leadership.* The Wallace Foundation. https://www.wallacefoundation.org/knowledge-center/pages/the-role-of-assistant-principals-evidence-insights-for-advancing-school-leadership.aspx

Gordon, S. P., & Ronder, E. A. (2016). Perceptions of culturally responsive leadership inside and outside of a principal preparation program. *International Journal of Educational Reform, 25*(2), 125–153. https://doi.org/10.1177/105678791602500202

Grissom, J. A. (2011). Can good principals keep teachers in disadvantaged schools? Linking principal effectiveness to teacher satisfaction and turnover in hard-to-staff environments. *Teachers College Record, 113*(11), 2552–2585. https://doi.org/10.1177/016146811111301102

Grissom, J. A., Egalite, A. J., & Lindsay, C. A. (2021). *How principals affect students and schools: A systematic synthesis of two decades of research.* The Wallace Foundation. https://www.wallacefoundation.org/knowledge-center/pages/how-principals-affect-students-and-schools-a-systematic-synthesis-of-two-decades-of-research.aspx

Grissom, J. A., & Harrington, J. R. (2010). Investing in administrator efficacy: An examination of professional development as a tool for enhancing principal effectiveness. *American Journal of Education, 116*(4), 583–612. https://doi.org/10.1086/653631

Grissom, J. A., Kalogrides, D., & Loeb, S. (2015). Using student test scores to measure principal performance. *Educational Evaluation and Policy Analysis, 37*(1), 3–28. https://doi.org/10.3102/0162373714523831

Guerra, P. L., Nelson, S. W., Jacobs, J., & Yamamura, E. (2013). Developing educational leaders for social justice: Programmatic elements that work or need improvement. *Education Research and Perspectives, 40,* 124–149.

Gümüş, E. (2015). Investigation regarding the pre-service trainings of primary and middle school principals in the United States: The case of the state of Michigan. *Educational Sciences: Theory & Practice, 15*(1), 61–72. https://doi.org/10.12738/estp.2015.1.2052

Gümüş, E. (2019). Investigation of mentorship process and programs for professional development of school principals in the USA: The case of Georgia. *International Journal of Educational Leadership and Management, 7*(1), 2–41. https://doi.org/10.17583/ijelm.2019.3718

Hafner, A. L., Allison, B., Jones, A., & Herrera-Stewart, I. (2012). Assessing the development of apprentice principals in traditional and residency programs. *Procedia – Social and Behavioral Sciences, 69,* 1134–1141. https://doi.org/10.1016/j.sbspro.2012.12.043

Harper, A. (2017, October 23). Shuffling principals can sometimes improve overall school district effectiveness. *K-12 Dive.* https://www.k12dive.com/news/shuffling-principals-can-sometimes-improve-overall-school-district-effectiv/507865/

Heller, R., Wolfe, R. E., & Steinberg, A. (2017). *Rethinking readiness: Deeper learning for college, work, and life.* Harvard Education Press.

Herrmann, M., Clark, M., James-Burdumy, S., Tuttle, C., Kautz, T., Knechtel, V., Dotter, D., Wulsin, C. S., & Deke, J. (2019). *The effects of a principal professional development program focused on instructional leadership* (NCEE 2020–0002). National Center for Education Evaluation and Regional Assistance; Institute of Education Sciences; US Department of Education.

Hess, F. M., & Kelly, A. P. (2007). Learning to lead: What gets taught in principal-preparation programs. *Teachers College Record, 109*(1), 244–274. https://doi.org/10.1177/016146810710900105

Hewitt, K. K., Davis, A. W., & Lashley, C. (2014). Transformational and transformative leadership in a research-informed leadership preparation program. *Journal of Research on Leadership Education, 9*(3), 225–253. https://doi.org/10.1177/1942775114552329

Hines, M. T. (2007). The effect of leadership style on preservice concerns about becoming a principal. *Educational Leadership and Administration, 19,* 103–149. https://files.eric.ed.gov/fulltext/EJ819952.pdf

Hoogstra, L., Hinojoso, T., Drill, K., Swanlund, A., Brown-Sims, M., Oliva, M., Manzeske, D., & Zajano, N. C. (2008). *Final report on the evaluation of the Texas Principal Excellence Program (TxPEP).* Learning Point Associates. http://www.air.org/sites/default/files/downloads/report/TxPEP_Final_Narrative_and_Appendices_0.pdf

Houchens, G. W., Hurt, J., Stobaugh, R., & Keedy, J. L. (2012). Double-loop learning: A coaching protocol for enhancing principal instructional leadership. *Qualitative Research in Education, 1*(2), 135–178. https://doi.org/10.4471/qre.2012.08

Howley, C., Howley, A., Yahn, J., VanHorn, P., & Telfer, D. (2019). Inclusive instructional leadership: A quasi-experimental study of a professional development program for principals. *Mid-Western Educational Researcher, 31*(1), 3–23. https://www.mwera.org/MWER/volumes/v31/issue1/V31n1-Howley-FEATURE-ARTICLE.pdf

Huang, T., Beachum, F. D., White, G. P., Kaimal, G., FitzGerald, A. M., & Reed, P. (2012). Preparing urban school leaders: What works? *Planning and Changing, 43*(1/2), 72–95. https://files.eric.ed.gov/fulltext/EJ977548.pdf

Hughes, A. L., Matt, J. J., & O'Reilly, F. L. (2015). Principal support is imperative to the retention of teachers in hard-to-staff schools. *Journal of Education and Training Studies, 3*(1), 129–134. https://doi.org/10.11114/jets.v3i1.622

Humada-Ludeke, A. (2013). *The creation of a professional learning community for school leaders: Insights on the change process from the lens of the school leader.* Sense Publishers. https://doi.org/10.1007/978-94-6209-320-1

Hunt, E., Haller, A., Hood, L., & Kincaid, M. (Eds.). (2019). *Reforming principal preparation at the state level: Perspectives on policy reform from Illinois.* Routledge.

Jacob, R., Goddard, R., Kim, M., Miller, R., & Goddard, Y. (2015). Exploring the causal impact of the McREL Balanced Leadership program on leadership, principal efficacy, instructional climate, educator turnover, and student achievement. *Educational Evaluation and Policy Analysis, 37*(3), 314–332. https://doi.org/10.3102/0162373714549620

Jacobs, J., Yamamura, E., Guerra, P. L., & Nelson, S. W. (2013). Emerging leaders for social justice: Negotiating the journey through action research. *Journal of School Leadership, 23*(1), 91–121. https://doi.org/10.1177/105268461302300104

James-Ward, C. (2011). The development of an infrastructure for a model of coaching principals. *International Journal of Educational Leadership Preparation, 6*(1), 1–12. https://files.eric.ed.gov/fulltext/EJ972967.pdf

James-Ward, C. (2013). The coaching experience of four novice principals. *International Journal of Mentoring and Coaching in Education, 2*(1), 21–33. https://doi.org/10.1108/20466851311323069

James-Ward, C., & Salcedo-Potter, N. (2011). The coaching experience of 16 urban principals. *Journal of School Public Relations, 32*(2), 122–144. https://doi.org/10.3138/jspr.32.2.122

Keiser, K. A. (2009). Educational administration candidates' diversity dispositions: The effect of cultural proficiency and service learning. *CAPEA Education Leadership and Administration, 21*, 59–71. https://files.eric.ed.gov/fulltext/EJ965156.pdf

Korach, S. (2011). Keeping the fire burning: The evolution of a university–district collaboration to develop leaders for second-order change. *Journal of School Leadership, 21*(5), 659–683. https://doi.org/10.1177/105268461102100502

Korach, S., & Agans, L. J. (2011). From ground to distance: The impact of advanced technologies on an innovative school leadership program. *Journal of Research on Leadership Education, 6*(5), 216–233. https://doi.org/10.1177/194277511100600508

Lackritz, A. D., Cseh, M., & Wise, D. (2019). Leadership coaching: A multiple-case study of urban public charter school principals' experiences. *Mentoring & Tutoring: Partnership in Learning, 27*(1), 5–25. https://doi.org/10.1080/13611267.2019.1583404

Lashway, L. (1999). Preparing school leaders. *Research Roundup, 15*(3). http://files.eric.ed.gov/fulltext/ED440468.pdf

Leithwood, K., & Jantzi, D. (2006). Transformational school leadership for large-scale reform: Effects on students, teachers, and their classroom practices. *School Effectiveness and School Improvement, 17*(2), 201–227. https://doi.org/10.1080/09243450600565829

Leithwood, K., & Louis, K. S. (2012). *Linking leadership to student learning.* Jossey-Bass.

Leithwood, K., Riedlinger, B., Bauer, S., & Jantzi, D. (2003). Leadership program effects on student learning: The case of the Greater New Orleans School Leadership Center. *Journal of School Leadership, 13*(6), 707–738. https://doi.org/10.1177/105268460301300606

Leithwood, K., & Riehl, C. (2005). What we know about successful school leadership. In W. Firestone & C. Riehl (Eds.), *A new agenda: Directions for research on educational leadership* (pp. 22–47). Teachers College Press.

Leithwood, K., Seashore Louis, K., Anderson, S., & Wahlstrom, K. (2004). *How leadership influences student learning.* The Wallace Foundation. https://www.wallacefoundation.org/knowledge-center/pages/how-leadership-influences-student-learning.aspx

Leung-Gagné, M., Levin, S., & Wechsler, M. E. (2022). *Developing effective principals: What kind of learning matters technical supplement.* Learning Policy Institute. https://learningpolicyinstitute.org/product/developing-effective-principals

Levin, S., & Bradley, K. (2019). *Understanding and addressing principal turnover: A review of the research.* National Association of Secondary School Principals; Learning Policy Institute. https://learningpolicyinstitute.org/product/nassp-understanding-addressing-principal-turnover-review-research-report

Levine, A. (2005). A race to the bottom: The nation's school leadership programs are not producing the educational administrators we need. *National CrossTalk, 13*(3). https://files.eric.ed.gov/fulltext/ED524422.pdf

Lindle, J. C., Della Sala, M. R., Reese, K. L., Klar, H. W., Knoeppel, R. C., & Buskey, F. C. (2017). A logic model for coaching experienced rural leaders: Lessons from year one of a pilot program. *Professional Development in Education, 43*(1), 121–139. https://doi.org/10.1080/19415257.2015.1037927

Lochmiller, C. R. (2014). Walking the line between employee and intern: Conflict in an administrative internship. *Journal of Cases in Educational Leadership, 17*(1), 72–83. https://doi.org/10.1177/1555458913518536

Lochmiller, C. R. (2018). Coaching principals for the complexity of school reform. *Journal of School Leadership, 28*(2), 144–172. https://doi.org/10.1177/105268461802800201

Lochmiller, C. R., & Chesnut, C. E. (2017). Preparing turnaround leaders for high needs urban schools. *Journal of Educational Administration, 55*(1), 85–102. https://doi.org/10.1108/JEA-11-2015-0099

Louie, B. Y., Pughe, B., Kuo, A. C., & Björling, E. A. (2019). Washington principals' perceptions of their professional development needs for the spike of English learners. *Professional Development in Education, 45*(4), 684–697. https://doi.org/10.1080/19415257.2018.1506353

Mann, D., Reardon, R. M., Becker, J. D., Shakeshaft, C., & Bacon, N. (2011). Immersive, interactive, web-enabled computer simulation as a trigger for learning: The next generation of problem-based learning in educational leadership. *Journal of Research on Leadership Education, 6*(5), 272–287. https://doi.org/10.1177/194277511100600511

Manna, P. (2015). *Developing excellent school principals to advance teaching and learning: Considerations for state policy.* The Wallace Foundation. https://www.wallacefoundation.org/knowledge-center/pages/developing-excellent-school-principals.aspx

Manna, P. (2021). How can state policy support local school districts as they develop comprehensive and aligned principal pipelines? *The Wallace Foundation.* https://www.wallacefoundation.org/knowledge-center/Documents/How-Can-State-Policy-Support-Local-School-Districts-Principal-Pipelines.pdf

Marshall, J. M., & Hernandez, F. (2013). "I would not consider myself a homophobe": Learning and teaching about sexual orientation in a principal preparation program. *Educational Administration Quarterly, 49*(3), 451–488. https://doi.org/10.1177/0013161X12463231

Master, B. K., Schwartz, H. L., Unlu, F., Schweig, J., Mariano, L. T., & Wang, E. L. (2020). *Effects of the Executive Development Program and aligned coaching for school principals in three US states: Investing in innovation study final report.* RAND Corporation. https://www.rand.org/pubs/research_reports/RRA259-1.html

McCotter, S. M., Bulkley, K. E., & Bankowski, C. (2016). Another way to go: Multiple pathways to developing inclusive, instructional leaders. *Journal of School Leadership, 26*(4), 633–660. https://doi.org/10.1177/105268461602600404

Militello, M., Gajda, R., & Bowers, A. J. (2009). The role of accountability policies and alternative certification on principals' perceptions of leadership preparation. *Journal of Research on Leadership Education, 4*(3), 30–66. https://doi.org/10.1177/194277510900400301

Miller, R. J., Goddard, R. D., Kim, M., Jacob, R., Goddard, Y., & Schroeder, P. (2016). Can professional development improve school leadership? Results from a randomized control trial assessing the impact of McREL's Balanced Leadership program on principals in rural Michigan schools. *Educational Administration Quarterly, 52*(4), 531–566. https://doi.org/10.1177/0013161X16651926

National Center on Education and the Economy. (n.d.). *NISL Program.* https://ncee.org/nisl-program/

New Leaders. (2018). *Prioritizing leadership: An analysis of state ESSA plans.* https://files.eric.ed.gov/fulltext/ED591503.pdf

New Leaders for New Schools. (2011). *The EPIC Leadership Development Program evaluation report* (Research Brief). https://files.eric.ed.gov/fulltext/ED533493.pdf

Ni, Y., Rorrer, A. K., Pounder, D., Young, M., & Korach, S. (2019). Leadership matters: Preparation program quality and learning outcomes. *Journal of Educational Administration, 57*(2), 185–206. https://doi.org/10.1108/JEA-05-2018-0093

Nunnery, J. A., Ross, S. M., Chappell, S., Pribesh, S., & Hoag-Carhart, E. (2011). *The impact of the NISL Executive Development Program on school performance in Massachusetts: Cohort 2 results.* The Center for Educational Partnerships at Old Dominion University. https://files.eric.ed.gov/fulltext/ED531042.pdf

Nunnery, J. A., Ross, S. M., & Yen, C. (2010). *The effect of the National Institute for School Leadership's Executive Development Program on school performance trends in Pennsylvania.* The Center for Educational Partnerships at Old Dominion University. https://files.eric.ed.gov/fulltext/ED531041.pdf

Nunnery, J. A., Yen, C., & Ross, S. M. (2011). *Effects of the National Institute for School Leadership's Executive Development Program on school performance in Pennsylvania: 2006–2010 pilot cohort results.* The Center for Educational Partnerships at Old Dominion University. https://files.eric.ed.gov/fulltext/ED531043.pdf

Orphanos, S., & Orr, M. T. (2014). Learning leadership matters: The influence of innovative school leadership preparation on teachers' experiences and outcomes. *Educational Management Administration & Leadership, 42*(5), 680–700. https://doi.org/10.1177/1741143213502187

Orr, M. T. (2011). Pipeline to preparation to advancement: Graduates' experiences in, through, and beyond leadership preparation. *Educational Administration Quarterly, 47*(1), 114–172. https://doi.org/10.1177/0011000010378612

Orr, M. T., & Barber, M. E. (2006). Collaborative leadership preparation: A comparative study of partnership and conventional programs and practices. *Journal of School Leadership, 16*(6), 709–739. https://doi.org/10.1177/105268460601600603

Orr, M. T., & Hollingworth, L. (2018). How Performance Assessment for Leaders (PAL) influences preparation program quality and effectiveness. *Journal of School Leadership and Management, 38*(5), 496–517. https://doi.org/10.1080/1363 2434.2018.1439464

Orr, M. T., & Hollingworth, L. (2020). *Designing performance assessments for school leader readiness: Lessons from PAL and beyond.* Routledge.

Orr, M. T., King, C., & LaPointe, M. (2010). *Districts developing leaders: Lessons on consumer actions and program approaches from eight urban districts.* Education Development Center, Inc. https://www.wallacefoundation.org/knowledge-center/documents/districts-developing-leaders.pdf

Orr, M. T., & Orphanos, S. (2011). How graduate-level preparation influences the effectiveness of school leaders: A comparison of the outcomes of exemplary and conventional leadership preparation programs for principals. *Educational Administration Quarterly, 47*(1), 18–70. https://doi.org/10.1177/0011000010378610

Ovando, M. N. (2005). Building instructional leaders' capacity to deliver constructive feedback to teachers. *Journal of Personnel Evaluation in Education, 18*(3), 171–183. https://doi.org/10.1007/s11092-006-9018-z

Parylo, O., Zepeda, S. J., & Bengtson, E. (2012). The different faces of principal mentorship. *International Journal of Mentoring and Coaching in Education, 1*(2), 120–135. https://doi.org/10.1108/20466851211262860

Perez, L. G., Uline, C. L., Johnson, J. F., Jr., James-Ward, C., & Basom, M. R. (2011). Foregrounding fieldwork in leadership preparation: The transformative capacity of authentic inquiry. *Educational Administration Quarterly, 47*(1), 217–257. https://doi.org/10.1177/0011000010378614

Pettus, A. M., & Allain, V. A. (1999). Using a questionnaire to assess prospective teachers' attitudes toward multicultural education issues. *Education, 119*(4), 651. https://link.gale.com/apps/doc/A55409983/AONE?u=anon~c7f5e087&sid=googleScholar&xid=7ce4bc52

Pham, L., Henry, G. T., Zimmer, R., & Kho, A. (2018). *School turnaround after five years: An extended evaluation of Tennessee's Achievement School District and Local Innovation Zones.* Tennessee Education Research Alliance. https://peabody.vanderbilt.edu/TERA/files/School_Turnaround_After_Five_Years_FINAL.pdf

Phillips, J. C. (2013). Revisioning a school administrator preparation program: A North Carolina case study. *Journal of Research on Leadership Education, 8*(2), 191–211. https://doi.org/10.1177/1942775113491412

Podolsky, A., Kini, T., Bishop, J., & Darling-Hammond, L. (2016). Solving the teacher shortage: How to attract and retain excellent educators. *Learning Policy Institute.* https://learningpolicyinstitute.org/product/solving-teacher-shortage

Reardon, S. F., & Hinze-Pifer, R. (2017). *Test score growth among Chicago public school students, 2009–2014.* Stanford Center for Education Policy Analysis. https://cepa.stanford.edu/content/test-score-growth-among-chicago-public-school-students-2009-2014

Reising, A., Orr, M. T., & Sandy, M. V. (2019). Developing beginning leadership performance assessments for statewide use: Design and pilot study results. *Planning and Changing, 49*(1/2), 93–114.

Rowland, C. (2017). Principal professional development: New opportunities for a renewed state focus. *The Education Policy Center at American Institutes for Research*. https://www.air.org/sites/default/files/2021-06/Principal-Profes sional-Development-New-Opportunities-State-Focus-February-2017.pdf

Rutledge, D., & Tozer, S. (2019). Policy transfer from local to statewide: Scaling evidence-based principal preparation practices in Illinois. In E. Hunt, A. Haller, L. Hood, & M. Kincaid (Eds.), *Reforming principal preparation at the state level: Perspectives on policy reform from Illinois* (pp. 62–88). Routledge.

Saleh, A., McBride, J., & Henley, J. (2006). Aspiring school leaders reflect on the internship. *Academic Exchange Quarterly*, *10*(3), 126–134.

Sappington, N., Baker, P. J., Gardner, D., & Pacha, J. (2010). A signature peda-gogy for leadership education: Preparing principals through participatory action research. *Planning and Changing*, *41*(3/4), 249–273. https://files.eric.ed.gov/fulltext/EJ952390.pdf

Sciarappa, K., & Mason, C. Y. (2014). National principal mentoring: Does it achieve its purpose? *International Journal of Mentoring and Coaching in Education*, *3*(1), 51–71. https://doi.org/10.1108/IJMCE-12-2012-0080

Shields, T., & Cassada, K. (2016). Examination of access and equity by gender, race, and ethnicity in a non-traditional leadership development programme in the United States. *School Leadership & Management*, *36*(5), 531–550. https://doi.org/10.1080/13632434.2016.1247050

Silver, M., Lochmiller, C. R., Copland, M. A., & Tripps, A. M. (2009). Supporting new school leaders: Findings from a university-based leadership coaching pro-gram for new administrators. *Mentoring & Tutoring: Partnership in Learning*, *17*(3), 215–232. https://doi.org/10.1080/13611260903050148

Simmons, J., Grogan, M., Jones Preis, S., Matthews, K., Smith-Anderson, S., Walls, B. P., & Jackson, A. (2007). Preparing first-time leaders for an urban public school district: An action research study of a collaborative district–university partnership. *Journal of School Leadership*, *17*(5), 540–569. https://doi.org/10.1177/105268460701700501

Soland, J., & Thum, Y. M. (2019). *Effect sizes for measuring student and school growth in achievement: In search of practical significance* (Education Working Paper No. 19–60). https://doi.org/10.26300/b5as-wr12

Spillane, J. P., Pareja, A. S., Dorner, L., Barnes, C., May, H., Huff, J., & Camburn, E. (2010). Mixing methods in randomized controlled trials (RCTs): Validation, contextualization, triangulation, and control. *Educational Assessment, Evaluation and Accountability*, *22*(1), 5–28. https://doi.org/10.1007/s11092-009-9089-8

Steinberg, M. P., & Yang, H. (2020). *Does principal professional development improve schooling outcomes? Evidence from Pennsylvania's Inspired Leadership induction program* (Education Working Paper No. 19–190). https://www.edworking papers.com/sites/default/files/ai19-190_0.pdf

Stevenson, C., & Cooner, D. (2011). Mapping the journey toward the principal-ship: Using standards as a guide. *Planning and Changing*, *42*(3/4), 288–301. https://files.eric.ed.gov/fulltext/EJ975997.pdf

Sutcher, L., Podolsky, A., & Espinoza, D. (2017). *Supporting principals' learning: Key features of effective programs*. Learning Policy Institute. https://learningpoli cyinstitute.org/product/supporting-principals-learning-key-features-effective-programs-report

Sutcher, L., Podolsky, A., Kini, T., & Shields, P. M. (2018). *Learning to lead: Understanding California's learning system for school and district leaders* (Technical Report). Getting Down to Facts II. Policy Analysis for California Education, PACE.

Thessin, R. A., & Clayton, J. (2013). Perspectives of school leaders on the administrative internship. *Journal of Educational Administration, 51*(6), 790–811. https://doi.org/10.1108/JEA-12-2011-0113

Tingle, E., Corrales, A., & Peters, M. L. (2019). Leadership development programs: Investing in school principals. *Educational Studies, 45*(1), 1–16. https://doi.org/10.1080/03055698.2017.1382332

Tucker, P. D., & Dexter, S. (2011). ETIPS leadership cases: An innovative tool for developing administrative decision making. *Journal of Research on Leadership Education, 6*(5), 250–271. https://doi.org/10.1177/194277511100600510

University Council for Educational Administration. (2008). *Advancing from preparation to leadership positions: The influence of time, institution & demographics.* http://3fl7ll2qoj4l3y6ep2tqpwra.wpengine.netdna-cdn.com/wp-content/uploads/2017/01/ImplicationsFeb2008.pdf

University of Illinois at Chicago College of Education. (2016). *Illinois board of higher education 8 year review self-study.* Department of Educational Policy Studies, Ed.D.

University of North Carolina Division of Academic and University Programs. (2015). *Great teachers and school leaders matter.* http://ncpfp.northcarolina.edu/wp-content/uploads/2016/09/UNC-Academic-and-University-Programs-Annual-Report-2015.pdf

Versland, T. M. (2016). Exploring self-efficacy in education leadership programs: What makes the difference? *Journal of Research on Leadership Education, 11*(3), 298–320. https://doi.org/10.1177/1942775115618503

Vogel, L. R., Weiler, S., & Armenta, A. (2014). Pushing back and forging ahead: Making principal preparation responsive to state and national changes. *Planning and Changing, 45*(1/2), 210–227.

Wang, E. L., Gates, S. M., Herman, R., Mean, M., Perera, R., Berglund, T., Whipkey, K., & Andrew, M. (2018). *Launching a redesign of university principal preparation programs: Partners collaborate for change.* RAND Corporation. https://doi.org/10.7249/RR2612

Wang, E. L., Schwartz, H. L., Mean, M., Stelitano, L., & Master, B. K. (2019). *Putting professional learning to work: What principals do with their executive development program learning.* RAND Corporation. https://doi.org/10.7249/RR3082

Wechsler, M. E. & Wojcikiewicz, S. K. (2023). *Preparing leaders for deeper learning.* Harvard Education Press.

Weiler, S. C., & Cray, M. (2012). Measuring Colorado superintendents' perceptions of principal preparation programs. *Educational Considerations, 39*(2). https://doi.org/10.4148/0146-9282.1116

WestEd, Learning Policy Institute, & Friday Institute for Educational Innovation at North Carolina State University. (2019). *Sound basic education for all: An action plan for North Carolina.* WestEd. https://www.wested.org/wp-content/uploads/2020/03/Sound-Basic-Education-for-All-An-Action-Plan-for-North-Carolina.pdf

White, B. R., Pareja, A. S., Hart, H., Klostermann, B. K., Huynh, M. H., Frazier-Meyers, M., & Holt, J. K. (2016). *Navigating the shift to intensive principal preparation in Illinois: An in-depth look at stakeholder perspectives* (IERC 2016–2). Illinois Education Research Council at Southern Illinois University. https://files. eric.ed.gov/fulltext/ED567016.pdf

White, E. D., Hilliard, A., & Jackson, B. T. (2011). Intentions and feedback from participants in a leadership training program. *Journal of College Teaching and Learning*, *8*(11), 51–58. https://doi.org/10.19030/tlc.v8i11.6508

Wiliam, D. (2011). *Embedded formative assessment: Practical strategies and tools for K–12 teachers.* Solution Tree.

Williams, S., Secatero, S., & Perrone, F. (2018). Preparing and developing leaders for indigenous-serving schools via the holistic blessing of POLLEN's leadership tree. *Journal of American Indian Education*, *57*(3), 27–50. https://doi. org/10.5749/jamerindieduc.57.3.0027

Wise, D., & Cavazos, B. (2017). Leadership coaching for principals: A national study. *Mentoring & Tutoring: Partnership in Learning*, *25*(2), 223–245. https://doi. org/10.1080/13611267.2017.1327690

Wise, D., & Hammack, M. (2011). Leadership coaching: Coaching competencies and best practices. *Journal of School Leadership*, *21*(3), 449–477. https://doi. org/10.1177/105268461102100306

Yirci, R., & Kocabas, I. (2010, April–June). The importance of mentoring for school principals: A conceptual analysis. *International Journal of Educational Leadership Preparation*, *5*(2).

Young, M. D. (2013). Is state-mandated redesign an effective and sustainable solution? *Journal of Research on Leadership Education*, *8*(2), 247–254. https://doi. org/10.1177/1942775113491260

Young, M. D., Crow, G., Orr, M. T., Ogawa, R., & Creighton, T. (2005). An educative look at "Educating School Leaders". *UCEA Review.* http://3fl71l2qoj 4l3y6ep2tqpwra.wpengine.netdna-cdn.com/wp-content/uploads/2013/11/ Spring2005.pdf

Young, M. D., Mawhinney, H., & Reed, C. J. (2016). Leveraging standards to promote program quality. *Journal of Research on Leadership Education*, *11*(1), 12–42. https://doi.org/10.1177/1942775116641086

Young, M. D., & Reedy, M. A. (2019). Statewide collaborations for improvement. In E. Hunt, A. Haller, L. Hood, M. Kincaid, & A. Duncan (Eds.), *Reforming principal preparation at the state level* (pp. 231–243). Routledge.

Zavitkovsky, P., & Tozer, S. (2017). *Upstate/downstate: Changing patterns of achievement, demographics, and school effectiveness in Illinois public schools under NCLB.* Center for Urban Education Leadership. https://urbanedleadership. org/wp-content/uploads/2020/02/UPSTATE-DOWNSTATE-FINAL-w-Appendices-06.16.17.pdf

Zepeda, S. J., Parylo, O., & Bengtson, E. (2014). Analyzing principal professional development practices through the lens of adult learning theory. *Professional Development in Education*, *40*(2), 295–315. https://doi.org/10.1080/19415 257.2013.821667

INDEX

Note: Page numbers in *italics* indicate a figure; numbers in **bold** refer to a table.